Revolution and
Rescue in Grenada

Revolution and Rescue in Grenada

AN ACCOUNT OF THE U.S.-CARIBBEAN INVASION

Reynold A. Burrowes

Contributions in Political Science, Number 203

Greenwood Press
NEW YORK • WESTPORT, CONNECTICUT • LONDON

Library of Congress Cataloging-in-Publication Data

Burrowes, Reynold A.
  Revolution and rescue in Grenada.
  (Contributions in political science, ISSN 0147–1066 ;
no. 203)
    Bibliography: p.
    Includes index.
    1. Grenada—History—American invasion, 1983.
I. Title II. Series.
F2056.8.B87   1988   972.98′45   87–23704
ISBN 0–313–26066–4 (lib. bdg. : alk. paper)

British Library Cataloguing in Publication Data is available.

Library of Congress Catalog Card Number: 87–23704
ISBN: 0–313–26066–4
ISSN: 0147–1066

First published in 1988

Greenwood Press, Inc.
88 Post Road West, Westport, Connecticut 06881

Printed in the United States of America

The paper used in this book complies with the
Permanent Paper Standard issued by the National
Information Standards Organization (Z39.48–1984).

10 9 8 7 6 5 4 3 2 1

Contents

Preface

Why did Grenada's Caribbean neighbors decide to invade Grenada?

Why were so many of America's staunch allies, so many members of Congress, and so many opinion leaders opposed to the U.S. response to a Caribbean request to lead an invasion against the tiny island of Grenada? And why did the U.S. people support it? Why did some Caribbean leaders and people support such a drastic step, while others did not? Were the vital interests of the United States threatened, as the president would have us believe, or was the Grenada invasion a means to restore American confidence in the uses of power, after America's humiliation in Vietnam, Iran, and Beirut? Was the president looking for an opportunity to act tough to boost his anticommunist image, while at the same time placating his right-wing critics who were complaining that his senior staff should "let Reagan be Reagan"? Was Grenada really the Cuban-Marxist satellite that the president would have us believe, or just a poor, tiny nation trying to gain the best for itself by playing the superpowers off against each other? Did Grenada's leaders start something that they could not control, or were they just a group of radicals of another banana republic who seized the government of a defenseless island?

The president of the United States told us, with photographs, that the airport being constructed in Grenada by the Bishop government was intended for Soviet and Cuban activity in the Caribbean. Why then were Britain and other European nations helping to finance its construction? Despite the concerns of the U.S. government, other allied governments thought that the project stood on its own merits and deserved their support. Didn't the U.S. president, the press, and others know this? Why had the U.S. public not known these facts before the invasion? Was the president of the United States misinformed? What was really going on?

This study was first conceived as a reaction to a speech given by President Reagan to the American nation. Being of Caribbean background and having maintained an interest in the area, I was astonished at the president's claim that the airport under construction in Grenada was for military use. One of the things I remember most from my travels to Grenada was its quaint airport.

I followed the subsequent development of the Reagan administration's rhetoric and Grenada's response in the press with renewed interest. Then came news of a coup in Grenada, the death of Bishop and of members of his cabinet, more stories of internal friction, the Caricom leaders meeting, and invasion.

My own reaction to these events was confusion. A few years ago my reaction would have been clear. Intervention was wrong, period. No reason could justify it. But now that it had happened so close to home, I began to see implications that I would never have considered before: the possibility of a prolonged civil strife, the death of innocent people as a small clique forced its way into power, and a dangerous precedent for other political hopefuls in the region. I was surprised at my own emotional and political reaction. Suddenly things were not as clear as they had been.

My purpose, therefore, in this study is twofold—first, to document what happened in Grenada and why, and second, to gain perspective on the motivations behind the actions and responses within the Caribbean region.

During the crisis and immediately afterwards, so much was written about the invasion that I thought my task would be easy. But as I began to write, gaps opened up. Perhaps because I did not realize how much work was required to close these gaps, I persevered to the end.

Acknowledgments

The sources from which I derived help are many. The *New York Times* and *Newsday* were indispensable sources, especially *Newsday*, which followed the developments before the United States became involved. The *Trinidad Guardian*, the *Express*, and Barbados's *Nation* and *Advocate* all did a superb job of covering the crisis from its inception. *The Times* of London and the *Observer* were essential supplements, possessing veteran reporters who know the area and the individual players well. In particular, the *Observer* provided a great deal of new information overlooked by metropolitan papers and was brilliant in its analysis.

I would like to record my deep gratitude to a number of friends who have helped me. The first is a person whose official position prevents me from mentioning her name. Her detailed knowledge of the politics of her country assisted me greatly in understanding the motivations and nuances of Grenada's politics and led me to many sources on the subject. Professor Benjamin Cohen of the Fletcher School of Law and Diplomacy is one of those academicians who is always busy with his own research, yet always finds time to read the work of his former students and friends even though his field is different from theirs. He came to New York to begin a sabbatical just as I was completing the first draft of this study, and he willingly agreed to my request.

Yvonne Toppin of the Barbados Consul General's Office in New York and Patricia Phillip of the Trinidad and Tobago Mission assisted me greatly with newspapers from those countries. Thanks go also to

Professor Kari Levitt of McGill University and Winston Macintosh, the Grenada scholar, for their comments and suggestions. Professor Anthony Appiah of Yale University gave me some insightful suggestions for changes in the structure and for further analysis. Bernadette Callerame Hodinar read and made several suggestions for the improvement of the first and final drafts and acted as a sounding board for my initial ideas. My thanks also go to my faithful editor and friend, Nancy Amy, who has again transformed my writing into readable prose.

My dear friend Ann Marche readily accepted the assignment to type for me for a second time. Her willingness to do so is indicative of her faith in my work and her generous nature. I would also like to thank Cathy Lore Potocki for typing and retyping the final draft of this study.

To these and the many others who have given me assistance, my sincere thanks.

Chronology

1498	Island sighted by Christopher Columbus during third voyage to the New World. He names it Concepcion.
1650	French settle the island, officially rename it Grenada.
1783	French cede Grenada to Britain. Most of the local Carib Indians have died. African slaves have been imported to work the large sugarcane plantations. ·
1833	Grenada made part of the Windward Islands Administration (British).
1951	Universal adult suffrage introduced.
1958	Windward Islands Administration dissolved. Grenada becomes member of Federation of the West Indies.
1962	Federation of the West Indies collapses. British colonial administration suspends constitution of Grenada. Chief Minister Eric Gairy charged with misuse of funds.
1967	Grenada becomes West Indies Associated State (WIAS) granted full autonomy over its internal affairs; Britain responsible for external affairs and defense.

1974 February	Grenada granted independence from Britain; Eric Gairy first prime minister.
1979 March 13	Eric Gairy overthrown in bloodless coup by Maurice Bishop, who becomes prime minister.
April 16	U.S. State Department warns Bishop of curtailment of U.S. aid if his close association with Cuba continues.
November 17	Bishop announces project to build new airport with help of Cuba; U.S.-Grenada relations worsen.
1980 May	Deputy Prime Minister Bernard Coard visits USSR.
November	Ronald Reagan elected president of the United States.
1982 April	Reagan complains to Caribbean prime ministers about Bishop and his involvement with the Cubans and Soviets.
July	Bishop visits USSR.
1983 March 23	Reagan's televised speech on Latin America shows reconnaissance photographs of Grenada airport under construction.
April 27	President Reagan, in address to joint session of Congress, again mentions Grenada and its potential for becoming key link for Soviet-Cuban and terrorist activities in Caribbean and Central America.
June	Bishop visits Washington, D.C., to mend fences; unable to set up a meeting with President Reagan. Meets with National Security Adviser William Clark and low-level State Department personnel.
September 14–16	New Jewel Movement (NJM) Central Committee meets to assess state of the revolution.
September 27	Central Committee members meet, pass resolution to split Bishop's duties with Bernard Coard.

September 28– October 8	Bishop departs Grenada for Czechoslovakia, Hungary, East Germany, and the Soviet Union with a stopover in Cuba on way home.
October 10	The People's Revolutionary Government (PRG), under Prime Minister Maurice Bishop, announces dates for public hearings on a new constitution being drafted by a special commission headed by Trinidad lawyer Alan Alexander.
October 12	Rumors begin circulating that two members of the government, Bernard Coard and wife Phyllis, are trying to kill Bishop; streets of St. George's empty as rumor spreads; Bishop, asked to ease tension, denies rumor on radio.
October 13	Meeting held to discuss joint leadership issue; Bishop accused of initiating rumor, expelled from NJM, and placed under house arrest. Crisis begins.
October 14	Rumors of an attempted coup in Grenada sweep through the Caribbean. Unconfirmed reports of Bishop and three cabinet ministers under house arrest. At noon Information Minister Selwyn Strachan announces Bishop replaced by Deputy Prime Minister Bernard Coard; at 3:30 P.M. government radio announces Bernard Coard has resigned.
October 15	At 11:00 A.M. Kendrick Radix, Minister of Agriculture, Fisheries, and Agro-Industry, leads a rally, urges crowd to support Bishop, and resigns as minister; arrested along with several others. No official report on crisis. Two cabinet ministers who support Bishop (Whiteman and Louison) meet Coard and Strachan to try to resolve crisis.

October 18   General Hudson Austin, Grenada's army
commander, gives account of events leading
up to crisis on Grenada State Radio; Unison
Whiteman announces resignation of five
ministers, including himself; students
protest—"no Bishop, no school."

October 19   Bishop rescued from house arrest by
supporters, subsequently killed along with
five other prominent NJM members; General
Austin announces that the army has
established a Revolutionary Military Council
that will form the government of Grenada. A
twenty-four–hour "shoot-on-sight" curfew is
imposed.

October 20   U.S. Marines rerouted from Middle East to
Caribbean.

October 21   General Austin lifts curfew to enable
residents to shop for basic supplies. The
Organization of Eastern Caribbean States
(OECS) meets in emergency conference in
Barbados to discuss Grenada situation;
leaders decide on invasion.

October 22   U.S., Canadian, and British diplomatic
officials from Barbados fly to St. George's
to investigate fate of their nationals in
Grenada and to assess situation.

October 22–23   Caribbean Community (Caricom) heads of
government meet in Port of Spain, Trinidad,
to discuss Grenada situation. Diplomatic and
trade sanctions imposed against Grenada.

October 25   U.S.-Caribbean invasion of Grenada begins.

October 27   President Reagan defends actions in Grenada
on U.S. television.

November 15   Interim government of Grenadian technocrats
appointed to guide Grenada until elections
are held.

Revolution and Rescue in Grenada

Introduction

The Caribbean area occupies a unique position within the Latin American region and indeed in the world. It comprises the only group of countries that were completely a creation of the entrepreneurial West. Almost all of its people were brought in by one phase or another of Western economic and commercial development—even the animals and plants in many of the islands were brought in by commercial interests. The islands and their societies were a commercial enterprise to serve as a source for tropical commercial agriculture, directed, owned, and controlled by the European powers that "created" them. Originally it was the sugar grown and produced in the Caribbean that provided the capital fueling the Industrial Revolution in England. However, since that time the islands have fluctuated between bust and boom as industrial market forces of the metropolitan capitals have become the main influence on their economies. Even sugar, a mainstay of many of these economies until today, has split its methods of production into an agricultural sector, where growing and harvesting continue to be done as they have been for 300 years, and a manufacturing sector, which is highly technical, requiring heavy capital investment.

The wealth generated in the period of the sugar boom never spawned a domestic entrepreneurial class as it did in the United States. Rather, successful Caribbean planters habitually returned to England to spend and invest their money, so that the acquisition of wealth in the Caribbean from its inception served only to facilitate the return to Europe for those who acquired it and serves to "emphasize their dependence on the outside markets where sugar was sold.'''[1] This loss of its most successful and innovative people impoverished an already artificial culture and society. In the case of Grenada, Eric Williams in his book *Capitalism and Slavery* shows that Britain's imports from New York between 1714 and 1773 totalled £1,910,796, while in ten short years between 1763 and 1773 her imports from Grenada totalled £3,620,504.[2] Because the islands themselves had no substantial indigenous culture and population from which to borrow or with which to intermingle, dependency on Europe was almost total. The customs of the slaves were judged by even the most sympathetic writers as merely quaint or interesting, not as possible social models. As a result, a culture was created that looked to Europe for economic, social, and political direction.

This pattern remained in the various colonies in different degrees until independence. But even within the European-dominated estate system, which did not provide much scope for creativity or for economic, social, and political development, the colonial peoples managed to improve their lot. Most often, however, West Indians have had to leave their island homes to find regular employment in order to fulfill their expectations for a better life for themselves and for their children. In a culture where education is stressed, this has meant the separation of parents and children for a prolonged period, or a wholesale uprooting of families.

West Indian labor has played a major role in the building of every major construction project undertaken by international business interests throughout the Caribbean basin area, from the building of the Panama railway in the 1860s and the Panama Canal down to the construction of the oil refineries in Venezuela in the 1940s and in Aruba and Curaçao in the 1950s. Indeed, Maurice Bishop was born in Aruba while his father was working on one such project, and his predecessor, Eric Gairy, worked on the same project as Mr. Bishop before returning to his native Grenada, where he entered politics. As a result of the constant movement and migration in search of jobs, West Indian society has been robbed of whatever continuity it might have possessed. This condition has repeated itself in the modern era with migration to Britain, Canada, and the United States and with the constant movement of professional groups in many islands as governments rise and fall or become less tolerant of professionals and others with opposing viewpoints as they seek to remain in office.

The growth of American influence in the area increased dramatically during and after World War II. By that time the United States had acquired a number of military bases from Britain in the islands and in Guyana. The rapid buildup and expansion of the tourist industry since then, together with the expansion of banking, bauxite mining, and light manufacturing, has taken many Americans to the area in different capacities. As a result, West Indians have come to hold a mixed view of the United States. This is how two historians have summarized that view:

West Indians knew that they had moved out of the orbit of Britain into that of the United States, and there is an obvious ambivalence in their attitude toward the cultural and economic influences exercised by so powerful a neighbour. They admire the egalitarian principles enshrined in the American constitution and they deplore the racial discrimination that still exists. They are impressed and attracted by the brilliant scientific and technological achievements of the United States, but they have no wish to become merely satellites. They like Americans and they make a great effort to attract them to their countries, but they are not prepared to accept the establishment of hotels that seek in any way to discriminate against their own people. They admire American wealth and business efficiency and they share the American conviction that educational opportunity up to university level should be available to anyone, but they are often apprehensive about American aid programmes with their heavy emphasis on the use of American expertise and American equipment.[3]

The United States is regarded by the people of the Caribbean with respect and admiration for its ideals and achievements, friendship for its generosity, and apprehension over its policies and social patterns. As a result, Caribbean people have a keen appreciation for the stated versus the operational policy of many aspects of U.S. life and behavior.

From the standpoint of foreign policy, the United States and the Commonwealth Caribbean have enjoyed relatively smooth relations, punctuated at times by short periods of difficulty with particular countries. These difficulties have most often been restricted to policy approaches to solving economic problems. But while Caribbean heads of government like Michael Manley of Jamaica and Maurice Bishop of Grenada have seen these as problems over which honest men can differ, U.S. administrations, particularly Reagan's, tend to view such differences as an affront and seriously in conflict with U.S. interests. This, in turn, breeds hostility and a relationship that leads the U.S. to take a partisan position in domestic politics, as it clearly did in Jamaica. American action in Jamaica was not that of a major superpower interested in maintaining good relations with all parties in a country, fostering confidence in a multiparty system, or promoting political alternatives and democratic change.

The situation in Jamaica was made more critical by the presence next door of Puerto Rico. While the Reagan administration openly favored one political party in Jamaica because of the administration's free enterprise philosophy, Puerto Rico was a failure of just such a system. Having been touted in the 1960s and 1970s as a model of free enterprise for the hemisphere, a decade later it has become a dismal economic failure with 23 percent unemployment, an extremely low growth rate, and a general decline of nearly every economic indicator.

The uncritical transfer of the U.S. economic system without regard for the lack of the domestic ability within other nations to maintain a high and continuing level of investment, given patterns of consumption and demography, condemned it to failure. And it is not as though there are not in the United States itself serious differences over emphasis and organization of its free enterprise system.

Many Caribbean scholars have argued for years that U.S. scholars and policymakers do not take the specific differences of Caribbean and Third World countries into account when advocating the simple transfer of a mature system that has developed out of very different circumstances. The modification proposed by Caribbean leaders of partnerships between government, business, and labor with strong central planning was anathema to the U.S. policymakers and especially to U.S. business. But if the United States was adamantly opposed to modifications to a system that had brought it so much success, many Caribbean scholars were equally adamant in their intention to pursue another course of development.

It is this situation that often brings men like Bishop into direct conflict with the United States. But Bishop, Manley, and others representing a modernizing middle class found in most developing countries are termed left-wing and radical, leaders with whom the U.S. administrations, Democratic and Republican, have found it difficult to deal. The rise of Japan, South Korea, Hong Kong, Brazil, Taiwan, Singapore, and other nations and the simultaneous decline of the U.S. industrial base have given some credence to those who have argued that the United States itself has failed to keep pace and modernize its own system and thinking. Perhaps the greatest failure of U.S. hegemony since the close of World

War II is that it has failed to win over the modernizing elite and the middle class of most developing countries from which most of the leadership in the Third World has come. The United States view of this group as leaning to the Left has created friction that has often stymied and frustrated the policies of both. Because U.S. scholarship in the area of economics and politics since 1945 has tended to support the U.S. government and its policy positions, relations have never really developed in the United States much beyond the point of talking past each other.[4] To a large extent this was a continuous undercurrent in U.S.- Grenada relations during the Bishop period. The actions of the Reagan administration were a stricter and more rigid application of the same principle. But under both Democratic and Republican administrations, U.S. policy has remained fairly constant.

It is ironic that America, the nation that lent its support to the decolonizing process by supporting the right to self-determination and by pressuring its European allies to give many of the developing countries their independence, should have expected these countries to so rigidly follow its economic and political example. It is also ironic that the United States, the nation that took the lead in ushering in the era of open diplomacy upon becoming a world power, has fallen back on the principles that had guided the older order. It has refused to recognize that we now have a "global system of international politics," where regions and subregions have their own peculiarities and insist on asserting their own interest, regardless of which major power they flirt with from time to time.[5] Again and again over the last two decades we have seen countries, written off by U.S. policymakers as firmly in this camp or that, do a complete turnabout without U.S. pressure, the most notable examples being Egypt and Guinea. We have also seen U.S. miscalculation lead to foreign policy blunders and embarrassment because of a simplistic belief that Third World leaders are always a surrogate for some other power. A recent example was Syria's involvement in the Lebanese crisis. It is hard to avoid the conclusion that U.S. policymakers have a certain contempt for Third World leaders, seemingly only because they insist on knowing and acting in their own interests and refuse to be led by more powerful states with which they may be allied. This tendency was noted by a prominent diplomatic historian some time ago:

Responsible British and American statesmen still commonly speak as if there were a natural harmony of interests between the nations of the world which

requires only good-will and common sense for its maintenance, and which is
being willfully disturbed by wicked dictators. British and American economists
still commonly assume that what is economically good for Great Britain or the
United States is economically good for other countries and therefore morally
desirable. Few people are yet willing to recognize that the conflict between
classes cannot be resolved without real sacrifices, involving in all probability
a substantial reduction of consumption by privileged groups and in privileged
countries. There may be other obstacles to the establishment of a new international order. But failure to recognize the fundamental character of the conflict,
and the radical nature of the measures necessary to meet it, is certainly one of
them.[6]

The Bishop government of Grenada fell into the category of a government that brazenly defied U.S. policy. Both the Democratic Carter
administration and the Republican Reagan administration objected to
that government's friendship with Cuba. But those close relations were
developed at a time when the precipitous rise in the price of oil and
two recessions in the United States severely reduced the amount of trade
and tourists flowing to the region. As a consequence, recession and
stagnation gripped the Caribbean and Latin America. Preoccupied with
its own domestic affairs and its more pressing foreign policy commitments, U.S. policymakers seemed to have little interest in the area until
they saw a decisive turn to the Left by a number of governments and
the threat of a number of insurgency movements against established
governments. By then, the years of political and economic neglect of
these small states had bred resentment and disappointment on both sides.

But most importantly, there had been a decline in the political situation in the Caribbean, leading to fear and uncertainty for those in
office. This was the situation that existed in the Caribbean islands close
to Grenada. Their declining economic condition made them much more
fearful of the influence of Grenada than they might otherwise have been.
They feared that the radical political element in their own countries
would adopt the New Jewel Movement method of attaining power.
They also feared that their high unemployment would provide the NJM
with the audience and recruits for radical politics. The moderate success
of the Grenada economy made these politicians even more anxious for
their own positions as left-wing parties throughout the area increased
their criticism of these governments with new zeal. The frustration and
desperation of some Caribbean governments was felt even more as the
recession of North America and Europe was turned into a depression

in the Caribbean area. High foreign exchange bills from oil imports, lack of foreign exchange earnings, stiff terms for borrowing from international agencies, and no policy for relief from the traditional aid donors in North America and Europe made the situation quite desperate. These were the reasons why the earlier response of the Caribbean governments to the Reagan administration's protest over Grenada was a demand for aid. Even after the Caribbean Basin Initiative was proposed, the response was to plead for a greater portion of the proposed allocation, so that even though there was support for Bishop among the different governments of the Commonwealth Caribbean, it was always qualified support because of the nature of that government and because its very existence was a potentially destabilizing force.

The attention paid to Grenada by the Reagan administration, which made no secret of its displeasure with that country's government, meant that it was seen as a maverick by most governments. As a result, even those governments that were sympathetic had to be very strong and sure of themselves in deciding to associate with Grenada. The simple knowledge that the Bishop government was in disfavor with the United States was sufficient to cause corporations, tourists, and governments to limit or simply not increase their trade and commercial relations with Grenada. The enormous power to influence others that the United States has as the preeminent economic, financial, and military power of the West can overwhelm most governments, especially those of small countries like Grenada. In the final analysis, though, it was Maurice Bishop and the NJM that ultimately made their choice of what direction to take, and they alone bear responsibility for the course that events took in their island nation.

Aware of their standing with the United States from the very beginning, they could have taken steps to insure their security and to minimize friction and internal conflict within their country and party. No external invading force killed Maurice Bishop and one-third of his cabinet—Grenadians did so. The system they themselves set up produced the machine that in the end consumed them. Once the internal struggle was brought into the streets, Bernard Coard and his friends should have anticipated the sort of measures their Caribbean neighbors would resort to. The possibility of prolonged disorder in Grenada could easily jeopardize the security of neighboring governments, and in view of the rumblings that had gone on before among radical groups, this was not a situation that they would tolerate for long. The neighbors were convinced that orderly government could not be restored by the Grenadians themselves without further bloodshed and were not prepared to allow this if they could avoid it. Even if the Revolutionary Military Council could have quickly asserted its right to govern, many of the Caribbean Community (Caricom) and Organization of Eastern Caribbean States (OECS) neighbors had already made up their minds that they would not do business with men who came to power in such a fashion. From a political and security standpoint, the Coard clique's handling of what started out as an internal party dispute was clumsy, shortsighted, and brutal. It also opened the door for NJM detractors and those who felt threatened to walk in.

For the United States, which had prepared itself for just such an eventuality, the timing of the crisis and the invitation to invade could not have come in a better package than from Grenada's OECS and Caricom neighbors. The invasion itself was a perfect mask for the failed policy of the Reagan administration in Lebanon; it was good for the administration's own domestic image preceding an election, and it also showed a sympathetic side that saw U.S. troops coming to save defenseless people from a small, ruthless clique. Still, after the selfish intentions of the Reagan administration and the OECS governments are discounted, one must reconcile the action of invasion with the desire of the people of Grenada and of the Caribbean generally to have someone do something about the brutal slayings in Grenada, the breakdown of law and order, and the possibility of further violence. While international law on intervention seems clear, its interpretation has always been thorny in relation to major powers with the ability to enforce their will on other states. The further question of when a government is legitimately constituted and recognized is also unclear.

On the night that the news of Bishop's murder was received by Grenadian officials in the United States, a number of senior government servants at the Grenada Mission in the United States held an informal meeting to debate what they should do. The debate ended hours later with senior civil servants deciding that the law as it stood gave them no recourse for action. They could not approach the UN because they were not the government of a country, and they could not approach other governments. Yet as they sat in discussion, they all knew that the army/radical group that had butchered their head of government and members of his cabinet was also not in control. The question was, Does force of arms make for international legitimacy? Does the possession of the airport, guns, and the radio station? At that time and for some time thereafter, no one was in effective control of Grenada, and those who tried were self-appointed and doing so on their own behalf. No other groups could have done so from Grenadian soil without risking loss of life and civil disruption; any group outside the country could speak freely, but had no opportunity to be in effective control.

This problem is not new, but it is one that governments and international organizations have ignored, partly out of self-interest and partly in recognition of its complexity. The situation in Grenada, where a small, unpopular clique seized power and held it by force of arms, begged for a solution. International relations required that answers be found, and the OECS countries and the United States acted as they had to. Regardless of its policy toward Grenada before the crisis, once the situation became as critical as it did, the United States had to respond, for otherwise a deep sense of despair might have descended on an already economically depressed region of the world.

NOTES

1. J. H. Parry and P. M. Sherlock, *A Short History of the West Indies*, 3d ed. (London, Macmillan 1980), p. 124.

2. Eric Williams, *Capitalism and Slavery*, as quoted in Hugh O'Shaughnessy, *Grenada*, p. 31.

3. Parry and Sherlock, *Short History of the West Indies*, p. 313.

4. David P. Calleo, *The Imperious Economy* (Cambridge: Harvard University Press, 1982), p. 90.

5. Geoffrey Barraclough, *An Introduction to Contemporary History* (London: Penguin, 1978), p. 103.

6. Edward Hallett Carr, *The Twenty Years' Crisis, 1919–1939* (New York: Harper Torchbooks, 1946), p. 237.

1

Politics in Grenada: Before the Revolution

The island of Grenada is the southernmost of the Windward Islands in what used to be the British West Indies. It was sighted by Christopher Columbus in 1498, although neither the Spanish, the dominant power in the area at that time, nor the British, the growing power to whom it was granted in 1627, settled the island. Eventually it was purchased by the governor of Martinique in 1650 and passed into the hands of the French West India Company in 1665, which then administered it until the company was dissolved in 1674. At that time the island reverted to the French Crown. The island was captured and recaptured by French and British forces as European powers vied for supremacy in the area. Eventually it was ceded to the British in 1783 by the Treaty of Versailles.

Grenada has 110,000 people, most of whom are of African descent, with a small population of mulattoes and East Indians. The Carib Indians who originally inhabited the island are extinct. Because of its main crops—nutmeg, bananas, and cocoa—the economy of Grenada has tended traditionally to do relatively better than those of the other, sugar-growing Caribbean Islands. As in its sister Caribbean countries, nationalism gained strength on the island after World War II.

T. A. Marryshow, self-educated journalist and politician, is credited with almost single-handedly arousing the political consciousness of the population and mobilizing the more educated urban middle class to oppose British colonialism and to press for adult suffrage and representative government. But the policy of dialogue and negotiation was discredited when the colonial government treated these demands with a politeness just short of disrespect. In the early 1950s Eric Gairy concentrated his energies on union organization and representation among the agricultural workers. His success as a unionist was swift and helped win him the loyal support of the rural workers and peasant farmers. The Grenada National Party (GNP), headed by Herbert Blaize, arose mainly as opposition to the Grenada United Labour Party (GULP) and has remained largely so.

These were the two dominant political groups at this time. In an attempt to prepare the island for self-government and then independence, the British instituted a new constitution in 1951, giving the island representative self-government. Universal adult suffrage was granted, allowing everyone over the age of twenty-one to vote. Elections were duly held, and for the next twenty-eight years two men vied for the country's leadership: Eric Gairy and Herbert Blaize.

GULP (Gairy) 1951–1957

GNP (Blaize-Thomas coalition) 1957–1960

GULP (Gairy) 1960–1962

GNP (Blaize) 1962–1967

GULP (Gairy) 1967–1972

GULP (Gairy) 1972–1976

GULP (Gairy) 1976–1979

NJM (Bishop) 1979–1983

In 1957 Eric Gairy was disenfranchised by the British colonial administration for personally leading a disruptive steel band demonstration through an open-air political meeting of another party. When Gairy's United Labour Party was re-elected in 1960, he proceeded to run the government in such a loose, unaccountable fashion that the British charged him with ''squandermania.'' Elections were held again in 1962; Blaize and his Grenada National Party were elected largely because of a promise to seek unitary statehood with Trinidad and Tobago. Blaize was the very antithesis of the free-spending, flamboyant Gairy. But when his unitary statehood failed, Gairy was once more returned to office. While out of office, Eric Gairy had had a serious struggle to keep himself afloat financially. His supporters claim that the experience had a profound effect on his character. His priorities seemed to have shifted to the acquisition of personal wealth and power. Despite a tendency to autocratic rule, he retained a strong political base, especially among the rural farmers and agricultural workers.

Many people in the urban areas, however, did not support Gairy and his United Labour Party. They resented his lack of educational preparation for office and his preoccupation with self-aggrandizement; aggressive in his flamboyant style, he never fully won the confidence of this group. However, having come from a poor background and having championed the cause of the agricultural workers and farmers, he continued to maintain a high standing among rural workers, who were generally distrustful of the educated urban professionals because they had not paid attention to their plight before.

Even before the British had officially departed, Eric Gairy moved to insure that his party remain the preeminent political party by pressuring opinion leaders to join him. Gairy and his United Labour Party employed his ''mongoose gang,'' a group of staunch party supporters who volunteered to discipline by force those who actively opposed them. The group had gotten its name when a number of these men had been temporarily employed by the Ministry of Health some years earlier to rid specific areas of mongoose infestation. Although the gangs had no official status within the party, the electorate knew of their existence, but only party activists of the opposition were targets of the gang, and, as a result, the public did not concern themselves with them. So loose was their affiliation to the party that the gangs sometimes challenged and fought each other.

A number of professional people who had originally supported Gairy, hoping to provide a stabilizing influence to his personality, disagreed with his increasingly arbitrary manner, his treatment of the opposition, and the way he conducted state affairs, and so parted company with his government. This disagreement deepened after a number of laws were passed for the purpose of muzzling and frustrating opposition.

The Public Order Act made it illegal for anyone to use a public address system without a permit from the commissioner of police. Naturally, the only persons to whom permission was given were Eric Gairy and members of his United Labour Party. The Police Amendment Act allowed the police to arrest and hold people without charge for forty-eight hours. The act was used to arrest and rearrest opponents continuously. The Firearms Amendment Act was used as an inducement to woo businessmen, by promising permits in return for their support, and other opinion leaders had their guns taken away if they did not support

Gairy. The Publications Amendment Act prohibited the importation of literature that the government labelled undesirable. It also forbade publication of periodicals issued more often than every three months (one hundred days) apart without the government's permission. This made it virtually impossible for any opposition group to put out any literature.

The Newspaper Act forbade the printing and publishing of a newspaper without a $20,000 deposit in the government's treasury. This act was passed after a number of political papers appeared, many carrying libelous statements and articles against the government and Gairy in particular. He sued one paper and won, only to have it declare bankruptcy. Incensed that the law could be used to benefit others as well, he had the act passed to correct this political problem, but it also muzzled the established editors, who were thereafter more cautious in their criticism and writing.

The style of the old opposition parties and the position they took did nothing to seriously challenge Gairy's power or his political base. Furthermore, they failed to attract many young people to their side as they continued to lose to Gairy in successive elections. It was not until a new generation of university-trained young people returned in sufficient numbers to their island home that active political organizing and discussion was revived in the late sixties and early seventies.

Oddly enough, the new generation's baptism into public politics did not have its genesis in Grenadian politics. It was the arrest of Grenadian citizens in Trinidad, a sister Caribbean country, during Black Power demonstrations in early 1970 that led a recently returned young lawyer named Maurice Bishop and others to organize a number of demonstrations to support and defend fellow Grenadians caught up in that protest.

Maurice Bishop was born on May 29, 1944, in Aruba to Grenadian parents. His parents returned to Grenada a few years after he was born, and his father became a successful merchant. Bishop attended secondary school on the island, then left for London to study law in 1963. Three years later he was admitted to the bar at Gray's Inn in London.

As a student, Bishop was active in student politics and became head of the West Indian Student Society. At the end of his studies, rather than return home as many other student leaders he knew were doing, he decided to remain in London. There he took up a relatively minor civil service job with the London County Council and helped set up the Legal Aid Society in Notting Hill Gate, a section of the slums of London where many West Indians lived and which had been the scene of racial

violence a decade earlier. Here Bishop experienced the deprivation of
the West Indian colony in a dreary part of London, which he could
contrast with the aspirations of his fellow Caribbean students who were
destined to become the future leaders of the Caribbean.[1] London for a
young ambitious black was not promising in terms of building a career,
however, so he decided to return home to Grenada in 1969.

There he opened a practice of his own and quickly became known as an
able attorney with a bright future. He had been home only a short while
when in 1970 he attended a meeting of West Indian political activists and
ideologues held on Rat Island off the coast of St. Lucia to discuss Black
Power and the prospects for further change in the Eastern Caribbean. The
participants in the Rat Island meeting formed the Forum group, "a loose
grouping of reformers who agreed to keep in touch with one another, as
they pursued their own political aims in their respective islands."[2] Back
home in Grenada Bishop organized a Forum group to protest against the
policies of the Gairy government. One act that brought the group into
prominence was its protest against the arrest of several Grenadians in
Black Power demonstrations in Trinidad and the failure of the Grenada
government to do anything to help them. But the group, never more than
a few members, fell away quickly. Within a short while Bishop, along
with a small group of friends, formed another organization, the Movement for the Advance of Community Effort (MACE), which was committed to the annual commemoration of African Liberation Day. This
idea had its genesis with the African Society for Cultural Relations with
Independent Africa (ASCRIA) in Guyana with the help of an Afro-Amer-
ican group from the United States that had recommended that celebrations be held throughout the Caribbean on the same day. These modest
political efforts brought Bishop increasingly into the public view.

A protest for better conditions for nurses at the St. George's Hospital
in November 1970 was the first opportunity for the new group to engage
in serious political activity against the government, and their action was
met with a stern response. The demonstration by the nurses, which was
joined by MACE and other groups, was broken up by police using tear
gas, and a number of people including Bishop were arrested. Bishop and
another young associate, Kendrick Radix, agreed to defend the twenty-
two nurses who were to stand trial. But their arrest was turned to good
fortune: they were joined by several lawyers from other islands in the
Caribbean who volunteered to help in the nurses' defense. The young
lawyers of MACE used the protracted length of the trials to show their

skill in the courtroom and to further challenge the government,and in the process they gained wide publicity for themselves and their cause. This experience seems to have given Bishop new political confidence. Shortly after, he and Radix came together to form a new political organization called the Movement for Assemblies of the People (MAP). Developing almost simultaneously was "the Jewel," the Joint Endeavor for Welfare, Education, and Liberation. Its members had organized a library, established a co-op farm, and published a weekly newspaper. The most prominent members were Unison Whiteman and Teddy Victor. This group made a rather dramatic entry onto the Grenada national scene.

Lord Brownlow of Great Britain was owner of the La Sagesse estate in the parish of St. David's. At the time of its purchase, the estate had by custom provided access to the public beach that bordered the property. Lord Brownlow first built a splendid mansion on the property, then cut off public access to the beach. This had the effect of making the beach virtually private, as most villagers had no way of gaining access to it. After the public outrage at this act got no attention from the government, JEWEL arranged a protest and a "People's Trial" of Lord Brownlow in absentia. The expatriate English landlord was found guilty of denying poor farmers their rights to the beach for the sake of his private vacations. News of the protest and the trial travelled quickly throughout the island, drawing attention to this group that served and identified with a rural part of the island.

But Eric Gairy and his party were not about to allow political neophytes to dominate any political issue for long. He moved decisively to outdo JEWEL in any objections it raised. In the case of the Brownlow affair he moved to acquire on behalf of the government and people of Grenada some thirty-two estates owned by expatriates on the island, including Lord Brownlow's La Sagesse estate. In doing so, he used an ordinance that had been placed on the books by none other than the British colonial administration. Eric Gairy and his Grenada United Labour Party could then boast that it was they who presided over the biggest social and economic revolution in Grenada's history.

Another group, which began much earlier but which only functioned when its main organizer visited Grenada from his teaching base in Trinidad, was the Organization for Revolutionary Education and Liberation. Most of the members of the OREL group came from Presentation College and St. Joseph's Convent, the best Catholic secondary schools on the island. At these schools the brighter senior students were

encouraged to take a leadership role in helping to plan the activities of the schools and the church. One document around which there was much debate was the implementation of the decisions of the Second Vatican Council.[3] It was this group that Bernard Coard befriended, then constituted as OREL and interested in the study of Marxism-Leninism, and for which he became the equivalent of the dean of studies. And it was this group that he later brought into the New Jewel Movement. While all of these groups had somewhat differing philosophies, they were united in their desire to see Eric Gairy and his Grenada United Labour Party out of office. This desire caused the three groups, MAP, JEWEL, and OREL to merge on March 11, 1973, to form the New Jewel Movement (NJM) with Maurice Bishop and Unison Whiteman as joint coordinating secretaries.

In retrospect, it is interesting that from its inception the NJM had no single leader and saw the leadership role as one of coordination. Initially this was the arrangement most preferred because it served the purpose of the small groups that came together to constitute the NJM. However, the party did not grow from group to organization, developing into a cohesive unit with areas of responsibility clearly demarcated. Rather, it was Bishop's charismatic personality that held a number of contradictory elements together, and this led to a heavy reliance on his presence to make things work.

The consolidation of these new groups into the NJM gave the opposition a greater visibility and greater strength to face the government. But New Jewel had a problem: the people did not flock to its banner as anticipated. Rather, some accused Bishop and his cohorts of being privileged children of the well-to-do and the middle class, intent on "challenging Gairy and the two-party system, which had worked well," for their own ends.[4] As a result, NJM was more popular in the urban areas among the youth, while Eric Gairy and his United Labour Party continued to be popular in the rural areas.

But the conflict between the New Jewel Movement and the government was one between generations also. The United Labour Party and the Grenada National Party were headed by men who came from the World War II generation and who had run the island for nearly thirty years. They were self-made men, many of whom, including Gairy, had never attended secondary school. They were nationalists who had gained a broad experience in the unions and as anticolonial activists. Maurice Bishop and many in the leadership of the New Jewel Movement had

benefited from the programs and improvements resulting from the agitation of these men.

While the achievements of unlettered Caribbean nationalist politicians are not belittled, these men have traditionally lost power and popularity very quickly once the scholar/politician arrives on the scene. This trend gave the NJM leadership confidence, but it also made them impatient to assume power. To capitalize on this predisposition of the Caribbean people is the hard work of political organization. However, among the population is a group that does not easily give up its beliefs and loyalties and is difficult to woo.

Shortly after its formation in March 1973, the NJM gained public attention through its activism in Grenville. The police in that city had shot and killed a man named Jerry Richardson. After getting little satisfaction concerning the details of his death from the police or government officials, his relatives sought the assistance of NJM leaders. The NJM leaders were outraged at the injustice of police acting with impunity and probably also sensed an opportunity to confront and embarrass the government. The deceased was buried with much political fanfare. NJM then staged demonstrations demanding the arrest of the policeman who had murdered Richardson, including an attempt to halt air traffic at Pearls airport. This caused the police to take action including rifle fire to prevent the demonstrators from invading the airport and runway. Their protest gained the government's attention, and the government, in turn, appointed an officer of the Trinidad and Tobago police force to conduct an inquiry. Some five months later the incident ended when the policeman responsible was prosecuted, convicted, and sentenced for murder. The incident launched the New Jewel Movement and set it up as a party ready to oppose the government. One fact uppermost in the minds of the NJM leadership was the announced intention of Eric Gairy to seek total independence from Britain. They had the strong feeling that once independence was obtained by Gairy, they would have little chance to engage in a political campaign and even less chance of winning. They knew that the British government was intent on giving its colonies independence as soon as they would have it, so as to be rid of the legacy and taunts of being called a colonial master and imperialist power at the UN and in other forums. The most that Bishop and his colleagues hoped for was sufficient delay of independence to allow them to organize an effective opposition and to capture the government. If the government thought that the appointment

of the inquiry and the subsequent conviction and sentencing of the policeman demonstrated its willingness to see justice done and would satisfy the NJM for a while, it was wrong. NJM's victory seemed to have emboldened it to take further action.

On November 4, 1973, the NJM held a political meeting at Seamoon in the parish of St. David's. The meeting was called a People's Congress. At the congress, a resolution was passed entitled "The People's Indictment." The congress directed the secretary of the NJM, Esley Carberry, to write to Eric Gairy, all of the ministers of his government, and all of the members of the Senate calling upon each of them to resign effective on November 18, 1973. He was also directed to enclose a copy of the resolution passed at the congress laying out the NJM's charges against the government. A list of the NJM's grievances against the government was presented under the heading "Major Crimes" comitted by the government against the people. The resolution read in part as follows:

1. The Gairy Government encouraged and openly condoned the murders of our citizens: viz. Bro. Jerry Richardson, Bro. Cummings, Bro. Lester Richardson, and Bro. Alister Saunders, among others.

2. The Gairy Government ordered or condoned the shooting of the ten peaceful and unarmed demonstrators who were protesting the murder of Jerry Richardson by a member of the Police Force. . . .

27. The Gairy Government has consistently neglected throughout its years in office from 1951 onwards the basic needs of the people for decent housing, adequate clothing, reliable transport, cheap and high quality medical facilities, a better quality of education for all our children, the development (instead of destruction) of our Agriculture for us to feed all of our people and the denial of the opportunity to work and earn a livelihood to over half of the people. These are the gravest crimes of which any Government can stand accused and be proved guilty.

And WHEREAS the PEOPLE of Grenada have now decided that for the reasons given above we must decide on the best course of action now open to us to save Grenada. NOW THEREFORE BE IT RESOLVED that a Congress of the People Meeting at Seamoon on the 4th day of Nov. 1973 has democratically and collectively agreed to take the following actions:—

(a) To pass a verdict of guilty on the charges laid against this Government and to condemn this Government for irresponsibility, corruption, incompetence, inefficiency, breach of contract, and to pass a vote of no confidence in the Government;

(b) *To call upon this Government to resign with effect from 18th November,*
    1973;

(c) To appoint a National Unity Council from among persons present at
    this Congress charged with the responsibility of implementing the
    decision taken at the Congress to remove this Government of the People
    pending the call of New Elections by the Governor to elect a new
    Popular Government;

(d) To agree to use the New Jewel Movement's "manifesto for power to
    the People" as the basis of a new plan that the new Government will
    operate to run the country.[5]

The resolution was a barefaced attempt by a fledgling political party
to wrest power from an administration for which it had little respect
and which it was eager to replace. But Eric Gairy and his Grenada
United Labour Party had been on the political scene for some time, had
been elected numerous times, and were not about to be displaced by a
group of young people because they willed it. In addition, whether they
liked it or not, Gairy headed the officially elected government, over
which there was no dispute at that time, and he emerged as the clear
leader, having gained an overwhelming majority at the polls. Since the
NJM leaders had never been elected to any post except within their
own party, the NJM resolution seemed abrasive and disruptive, and it
did succeed in incurring the government's wrath.

Later it was discovered by Gairy that some fifty .303 World War I
police rifles had been stolen from Presentation College, and there were
rumors that arms and ammunition were being smuggled into the island.
In an effort to deal with the NJM's threat to his plans and his power,
Eric Gairy, as the person charged with the responsibility for national
security, moved to implement some changes. He decided to strengthen
the police by employing a large number of able-bodied men as aides
to the police. It was well known that these police aides were staunch
supporters of Gairy's own party and members of the mongoose gang.
Although initially these police aides were to be employed and directed
by the regular police officers and sub-officers, having no legal standing
under the law, this understanding soon broke down.

The following weekend the NJM's weekly newspaper the *New Jewel*
of November 9, 1973, carried a front-page article that announced:

Congress Decides
1. Government guilty of 27 major crimes against the people

2. Government to go by November 18, 1973
3. On a National Unity Council to supervise the changeover of government
4. On the plans the New Government will carry out
5. On the steps the people will take to remove the government after November 18, 1973.[6]

The paper also made it clear for the first time what steps were to be taken if the government did not give in to the demand to resign. The people of Grenada would be called upon to support a general strike and other political activities. This is how the NJM paper broke the news of the decision and intended activity to the people:

The National Unity Council chosen at the Congress has already sent letters to Gairy, his 12 stooges in the House of Representatives, and his 9 lackeys in the Senate calling on them to resign. A letter has also been sent to the Governor and we expect her to use her powers under the constitution to make sure the Government gets off our backs and out of our lives before the 18th.

After further berating the government, the article went on to spell out in detail how the NJM planned to implement its threat to be disruptive:

To show our determination and seriousness to rid ourselves once and for all of the plague of Gairy's dictatorship, We The People will shut down the island completely, refuse to work, refuse to pay taxes, come out in the streets in tens of thousands, inform the world of our struggle for freedom, and generally do everything necessary to save our island from total destruction. We are confident that this will happen because we can see, feel, sense, and hear the New Fighting Mood of the people.

Gairy and his pack of paper tigers can never stand up to our determination and seriousness. Neither tear gas, nor searches, nor jail, nor guns can stop us.[7]

Together with this public show of hostility and aggressiveness toward the government, a number of rumors began to circulate as to what the NJM intended to do next to wrest power from the government. The most serious of these was that the NJM planned to overthrow the government by force if need be. To many Grenadians these acts by the NJM seemed to be reckless and irresponsible. Although they were not enchanted with Gairy, many disliked the abrasive and cantankerous style of the new party. Others interpreted its actions as a ploy to cause the government to lose its nerve. As NJM activism intensified, the government became more uneasy, not for fear of losing popular support, but for fear that NJM might precipitate a civil disturbance that would embarrass the government.

On November 18, 1973, the day that the NJM had set for the government to resign, the leading members of the party travelled to Grenville, where Maurice Bishop and one of the executives of the NJM were invited by Mr. H. M. Bhola to speak to a meeting of businessmen at the DeLuxe Cinema at 3:00 P.M. That a group of businessmen would consent to listen to the plans of this group intent on toppling the government or causing serious embarrassment to it was cause for concern. By this time the government was making preparations for independence from Britain and did not want any domestic political strife to interfere with its plans. The NJM, for its part, feared that once independence was achieved, there would be no way of getting a fair election fight against the governing United Labour Party, for there would be no one to oversee possible election fraud, which they were convinced would be committed, and no one to appeal to, as they were certain that the courts were compromised.

The government was equally determined that its plans for achieving independence would not be thwarted. Prior to their visit to Grenville on November 18, 1973, "Bloody Sunday," the leaders of the NJM were waging a single-handed campaign against the government with little success. Many deplored their abrasive style and inflammatory rhetoric and demands. Their visit to Grenville was an attempt to form an alliance with an important group that could be a valuable ally in their plans to make the political situation intolerable for the government to continue in office. But as it turned out, Bloody Sunday was an important watershed for politics in Grenada for all concerned, and hence events preceding and following demand some recounting.

Prior to the arrival of the NJM executives in Grenville, the police in that town had ''received information of a plan'' that the NJM planned to attack the Grenville police station as a preliminary step to displacing the government by force.[8] NJM executives Maurice Bishop, Kendrick Radix, Hudson Austin, Unison Whiteman, Selwyn Strachan, and Simon Daniel arrived in Grenville in two cars. They were prevented from entering the cinema and were beaten by police aides on the scene. Their cars were searched and it was alleged that arms and ammunition were found. They were arrested and thrown in prison. Even though it was obvious that some of their wounds were quite serious and needed medical attention, the police made no effort to get any medical assistance for the prisoners. When their relatives and friends, their lawyers, and a priest arrived at the station, the police still would not relent and allow them to get medical attention. All this time the police could not say on what charges they were being held.

Then they were charged and brought before the magistrate, who refused bail. The following day their lawyers appealed to another court and bail was granted. They were then immediately rearrested and charged under another section of the Firearms Ordinance that makes granting of bail discretionary. Upon appeal, the magistrate granted bail, even though the state opposed it. Despite this order by the courts, they were still held in custody. After a number of arrests and rearrests, the matter reached the Chief Justice, who ordered that the six be granted bail.

If this escalation of political activism by the NJM was an attempt by a group of desperate young men to prove that the government was all that they claimed it was, then they succeeded on Bloody Sunday. For while the acts of the NJM in the preceding weeks were clearly reprehensible, the response by the government officers to their actions was even more so. Their behavior showed the extent to which the police and other officers of the state were either in league with the political administration or were willing to go to prove their loyalty to the government.

When the news of the incident in Grenville became known, some party activists and supporters regarded the event as a continuing part of the usual interparty warfare that flared up from time to time. Many of these people regarded the NJM action of going to Grenville to organize politically inspired strikes and resistance in an area where the police were known to be exceedingly rough with lawbreakers generally and were particularly partial to the ruling party as provocative. Others saw them as a group of young upstarts intent on gaining power but not carefully calculating the consequences of their action. What was new was that professional men from the urban area had never been arrested before in that area in such numbers; for this reason the press chose to give their treatment some prominence.[9] But many among the urban middle class, including a number of prominent citizens who had managed to remain apolitical, were outraged, not so much at the violence itself, but at the implications that irregularities occurring in the police and judicial system had for the future of the society at large. As a result, a number of prominent individuals and civic leaders coalesced around the cause of the injured men. Petitions and complaints were collected and sent to the governor and to Premier Eric Gairy. They called themselves the Committee of Twenty-Two; churches, trade unions, the Chamber of Commerce, and numerous service clubs and civic organizations were represented, but no political groups. They were determined to press for an impartial commission of inquiry to investigate the entire Grenville incident. When the government did not give their concerns the weight they thought that it should, they called a general strike to show their seriousness. So impressive and united was this group in its determination to have an investigative commission that the government relented and appointed the Duffus Commission to investigate the incident.

The commission's findings were a severe blow to the government. It found that the Grenville police and police aides were themselves largely responsible for the violence they claimed to be trying to contain. After labelling the actions of the officer in charge, Inspector Belmar, as "those of a megalomaniac," the commission went on to say: "It was Belmar who had unleashed this Frankenstein on the town of Grenville and he was unable to control it." Referring to the activities of the police aides and the regular police themselves, it then stated: "In our view, Mr. Belmar proved himself to be totally unfitted for any position of authority."[10] The commission also found other government officers negligent in the way they carried out their duties. This is how it summed up its inquiry into the actions of two members of the judiciary: "We reject entirely the lame and untruthful excuses which were given by the Magistrate, Mr. Irving Duncan, and the Solicitor General, Mr. Nolan Jacobs. In our view, both men have shown themselves to be quite unfit for the responsible posts they hold."[11] The commission left no doubt that it found the political administration deeply implicated in the handling of the whole incident. Even though it believed that the government had good reason to worry about NJM activities, it could not sanction the government's handling of the affair.

The New Jewel Movement, realizing that it had captured the attention and sympathy of an important segment of the population, albeit temporarily, was determined to use it. Within days its members were back campaigning against the government. With the Duffus Commission still sitting, some thought that NJM would at least have awaited the outcome, but it did not. About two months after Bloody Sunday, on January 21, 1974, Dame Hilda Bynoe, the governor of Grenada, left the island hurriedly after Gairy had asked the queen to terminate Bynoe's appointment. She was one of a number of Grenadians who had returned to Grenada to work with Gairy, hoping to be a stabilizing influence on his administration. For months prior to her departure NJM members had picketed her residence weekly and included her in their name-calling when she did not respond to their petitions for assistance in their political struggle against the government. But her constitutional position permitted her to do little, and the NJM had no real case or constitutional grievance that was not being addressed anyway. The attacks on her were designed to have her take some action detrimental to her and the government. On that day also, Rupert Bishop, the father of Maurice Bishop, was shot and killed in a melee in St. George's. As the Duffus Commission was still sitting at the time the killing occurred, its terms of reference were widened to cover this new incident.

The Committee of Twenty-Two had accused the government of reneging on four matters agreed to earlier on November 27, 1973. Since it included among its ranks organizations representing both management and labor, the committee threatened a shutdown of all commercial and other services. Rather than seeming to capitulate once again to this group, Premier Gairy and his government passed legislation on January 3, 1974, designed to enforce the opening of the commercial establishments, with heavy fines for those who failed to comply.

Despite the new law, several commercial establishments remained closed on January 3, 1974. The Grenada Waterfront Workers Union and the Commercial and Industrial Workers Union, both headed by Eric Pierre, began a series of demonstrations on January 9 to show their solidarity and determination about the matter. The ranks of the demonstrators swelled with NJM members, who always welcomed an opportunity to show their displeasure with the government. As the commission put it: "We are satisfied that persons other than union members participated in them and that the opportunity was taken by persons opposed to the government to demonstrate their disfavor by songs disparaging to Mr. Gairy."[12] Nevertheless, the demonstrations themselves "were generally peaceful and offered no apparent threat to peace and good order." The government was worried that the new spate of demonstrations and public opposition to it could contribute to "preventing or delaying independence," a point not lost on many, including the political activists who inveigled their way into the demonstrations.

On the evening of January 21 the demonstrators returned to the union's headquarters, Otway House, to be addressed by the leadership. A number of police aides left Mount Royal, Premier Gairy's residence, and could be seen coming toward the open-air meeting. The crowd that had gathered outside parted and allowed the aides safe passage, but as the last aides cleared the crowd, a fight broke out. The police aides then turned on the crowd with everything from bottles and stones to gunfire. Many in the crowd retaliated. The melee went on in full sight of the regular police, who stood by and watched. Then they quite suddenly intervened with rifle fire and tear gas.[13] Mr. Bishop, who was sitting behind the door to keep unauthorized people out, was killed when a shot pierced the door behind which he sat and struck him. While the commission found that "Mr. Gairy had reasonable grounds to believe that the demonstrations involved political considerations which posed a threat to his leadership," they could not agree with the "measures to which he resorted in order to arrest its development."[14] They termed the attack by the police aides on the crowd and on Otway House an act of "unvarnished terrorism." The commission also noted that there was a "marked lack of candor among the senior ranks" of the police who testified before them. Of the incident itself the commission concluded that the police aides, "far from being heroic, fell far short of the type of resolute and spirited action expected of members of a disciplined force whose responsibilities deny them any manifest indulgence in partisanship, and whose paramount concern must be justice, the representation of the law and the maintenance of order."[15] After recognizing the perceived threat that Premier Gairy faced and observing that many of his political decisions were apparently based on reports by low-level security officers, it concluded that the causes of the riot were (1) gross negligence on the part of Mr. Gairy; and (2) the deliberate violent confrontation of the demonstrators by the police aides.[16]

About the police, the commission found that "members of the Police Force did not take any steps to prevent the riot; and when the riot occurred, they did not adopt any effective measures to control the conduct of persons involved in the riot. The use of rifle fire and tear gas worsened the situation."[17] The commission further noted: "The breakdown of discipline may be attributed to the insecurity among senior police officers and to their reluctance to assume individual responsibility for decisions involving action against the police aides.''[18] About the death of Rupert Bishop, the commission said nothing specific since it could not determine who actually fired the fatal shot. But while the NJM maintained that the police aides were responsible for Rupert Bishop's death, other impartial observers maintained that his wounds were more consistent with a shot from a police rifle. Although the commission proved the NJM right in asserting that the system had been so politicized as to make it nearly impossible for any other party to compete fairly for office, one point was lost in the euphoria at that time. This was that the government ultimately responded to political pressure and allowed the allegations to be investigated by an impartial commission under the law. As corrupt as the government might have been, in the face of organized and widespread objection the law of the land was enforced, even if just for a short while.

When the island was granted independence on February 7, 1974, Bishop and several of his colleagues found themselves under detention as the official celebrations were going on.[19] The conflict and confrontations continued until the general election of December 1976. In an effort to have the maximum impact possible at the polls, the New Jewel Movement formed an alliance with a number of groups, including the old opposition party, the Grenada National Party, and the United People's Party (UPP). The group called itself the People's Alliance. In his campaign Bishop told his audiences that the country was ready for a ''new political experience.'' When the results were read, Gairy's United Labour Party had nine seats (52 percent) and the People's Alliance coalition had six (48 percent).

Apparently stunned by the poor outcome, Bishop and his colleagues charged that the elections in the areas won by Gairy's party were rigged, but no real proof was offered to substantiate their charge, and according to several impartial observers, there had been no organized plan to steal the election from the People's Alliance. If there was any tampering at all, it was isolated and involved a handful of votes, which would not have had an effect on the final outcome.[20] But had the government not undermined the election commission, and had it given the press greater freedom, these charges might not have arisen, or they could have been refuted or dismissed more easily by an independent observer.

Within the Alliance a quarrel erupted over the way the seats broke down. Of the six seats the Alliance won, three were won by NJM members, two by UPP members, and one by the Grenada National Party leader. First there was the complaint that one of the seats won by an NJM member was a sure GNP seat that was sacrificed to the NJM. Within the NJM itself there was also some bad feeling. Seats were won by Maurice Bishop, Bernard Coard, and Unison Whiteman. Many within the party felt that Bernard Coard (who had not been resident in Grenada for very long) had not undergone any personal risk when NJM leaders were arrested and beaten and had been given a relatively safe seat by Bishop, while Bishop himself had stood for a marginal seat that only his political skill had helped him win by a handful of votes. But Coard had quickly proved himself to be a valuable asset as an ideologue and organizer to the leaders of the NJM, his most notable contribution being his almost single-handed writing of the party's manifesto. And Bishop, realizing that he lacked the administrative bureaucratic and organizational skills and the patience for the day-to-day running of a party, knew that he needed Coard.

Many saw the final result as a setback for Gairy and his United Labour Party, which lost its dominant position in Parliament. But most observers expect an incumbent government to lose some support over its tenure in office. The election proved that incumbents have a great advantage in an election. "They are there, and have to be displaced. Even unloved governments provide a measure of order and continuity to the context for everyday life. People do not readily abandon a stable order for the unknown."[21] But the result created a predicament for the NJM. They had no way of telling which faction had gotten what percentage of votes. NJM members actually took three seats, and they worried that the other members of the Alliance might leave with the other three. Many people interpreted the result as an anti-Gairy vote rather than a pro-NJM vote. Outwardly the NJM showed only signs of confidence, but inwardly they were disappointed that they had done so poorly.

Through his political activities Maurice Bishop had cultivated the friendship of many groups and politicians throughout the Caribbean. As an elected member of the Parliament of Grenada he travelled through the islands speaking to heads of governments, trade unions, church organizations, and other political groups about the situation in Grenada. He went so far in some of his talks as to remove his shirt to show the scars he had received while in prison. Sympathy for his cause grew as Gairy's repression of his opposition continued to intensify. By late February 1979 the government seemed determined to deal with the opposition more firmly. Bishop and other top officers of NJM went into hiding when it was learned that the security forces were carrying out extensive searches for them under the guise of searching for arms.

On Monday, March 12, 1979, Prime Minister Gairy left Grenada for New York via Barbados. Upon his departure, news circulated that he had left word that the leadership of the NJM be massacred in his absence. On March 13, 1979, convinced that their lives were in danger, a 70-man NJM group raided the high school armory for guns and knives and captured Gairy's 200-man Defense Force, inflicting only one casualty.

Many observers doubted that anything more than the usual detention, if anything, had actually been ordered, but in the absence of an independent press, rumors gain more credence and can be used by some to support their cause. The observers saw the NJM takeover as a move by a group of impatient young men and women, uncertain of their political support and eager to stage a coup at an opportune time.

Domestic reaction to the NJM takeover was one of shock and uncertainty. No one knew quite what to do, but people were glad that the political bickering was at an end and that the loss of life was minimal. Caribbean leaders reacted much the same. They were faced with a tough dilemma. They knew that Eric Gairy was eccentric and uninterested in government, desiring only the power, prestige, and lifestyle it afforded him. By this time Gairy had become fully eccentric, preoccupied with UFOs and other such phenomena rather than giving his undivided attention to the affairs of state. He was an embarrassment to many of his colleagues. But a coup was felt to be inconsistent with the traditions of the area and with all the principles the Caribbean people stood for. Never had there been a successful coup in the Commonwealth Caribbean, and the leaders hated to have a precedent set. But for the fact that Maurice Bishop was a member of Parliament, an opposition leader known to them, they might have completely rejected his government. For Britain and the United States, the two major powers with interests in the area, the overthrow of Sir Eric Gairy was no earth-shattering news; Grenada was but a speck in the ocean, and there were more important matters at hand.

NOTES

1. Hugh O'Shaughnessy, *Grenada: An Eyewitness Account of the U.S. Invasion and the Caribbean History that Provoked It* (New York: Dodd, Mead and Company, 1984) p. 43.

2. Ibid., p. 45.

3. Ibid., pp. 71–72.

4. Interview with former Senior Civil Servant.

5. Report of the Commission of Inquiry into the Breakdown of Law and Order and Police Brutality in Grenada, headed by Sir Herbert Duffus, 1975 pp. 57 and 60 (hereafter referred to as the Duffus Commission Report).

6. Duffus Commission Report, p. 133.

7. Ibid., p. 61.

8. Ibid., p. 19.

9. Interview with former Senior Civil Servant.

10. Duffus Commission Report, p. 25.

11. Ibid., p. 23.

12. Ibid., p. 216.

13. Ibid., p. 220.

14. Ibid., p. 219.

15. Ibid., p. 228.

16. Ibid.

17. Ibid., p. 229.

18. Ibid.

19. See the *Spectator*, London, October 29, 1983, p. 10.

20. Interview with former Senior Civil Servant.

21. William Pfaff, "Reflections" (Central America), *New Yorker*, August 15, 1983, p. 75.

2

After the Revolution

If Great Britain and the United States thought that the coup in Grenada was a domestic affair isolated on a tiny island and that it would take care of itself, they were mistaken. In today's world every nation has the potential to become a partner or problem.

The events in Grenada were not lost on one particular man in the Caribbean, a man who had been ostracized for a long time by the United States and the West and was looking for friends: Fidel Castro. He wasted no time in befriending Maurice Bishop and the new government of Grenada. He gave them help in tangible ways, supplying doctors, dentists, and teachers; and this, in turn, drew Bishop and his radicalized colleagues closer to Castro and his revolution.

Originally Bishop had appealed to everyone for help after assuming power. The United States, in whom the NJM, especially Bishop, seemed to place great hopes, gave no adequate response to his request. Rather, when U.S. Ambassador Frank Ortiz (accredited to the area but residing in Barbados) visited the island in April 1979, a few weeks after the NJM coup, he came to warn Bishop that the United States would not look with favor on any development of closer ties with Cuba. If the government of Grenada persisted, Ambassador Ortiz warned, it might result in a decrease in the flow of American tourists to the island.[1] He reportedly offered the government $5,000 in assistance. "This slap in the face," as NJM cabinet member Lyden Ramdhanny later characterized the offer, was perceived as a not-so-subtle attempt by the U.S. government to dictate what the new government could and could not

do. It was resented by the young NJM government, which was predisposed to look upon the United States with suspicion and was anxious
to show its independence and capability.

NJM was mistaken about the source of the money, as Ambassador
Ortiz's offer was not an official gift; rather, it was to be made available
from the embassy's own emergency fund. The official U.S. position at
that time was that all aid to the region had to be secured through the
Caribbean Development Bank or some other multilateral organization,
rather than through a government-to-government bilateral arrangement.

But the NJM felt insulted, and from that time on a "war of words"
between tiny Grenada and the United States began. In a speech delivered
three days after his meeting with Ambassador Ortiz, Maurice Bishop
gave a strong reaction to what he had been told:

We have always striven to have and develop the closest and friendliest relations
with the United States, as well as Canada, Britain, and all our Caribbean
neighbors. . . . But no one must misunderstand our friendliness as an excuse for
rudeness and meddling in our affairs, and no one, no matter how mighty and
powerful they are, will be permitted to dictate to the government and people
of Grenada who we can have friendly relations with and what kind of relations
we must have with other countries. We are not in anybody's backyard.[2]

Thereafter, the NJM government lived in constant fear of being overthrown or destabilized, directly or indirectly, by the U.S. government
or by one of its agencies. As a result, the government moved Left
toward a type of government Bishop and his colleagues might not have
anticipated a few months earlier when they assumed power. But it was
Fidel Castro's cunning in the face of U.S. nonchalance that pushed
Grenada to the center of world affairs.

Every government of Grenada over the preceding twenty-five years
had considered building an international airport, but none could summon
the will or arrange the financing for such a large undertaking. The NJM
in its manifesto had opposed the building of a new airport, categorizing
it as typical Third World emphasis on "prestige dream" projects and
citing the World Bank's own caution against an overly ambitious
project.[3] The NJM planned instead to develop and emphasize agriculture. But upon coming into office and finding a depleted treasury, it
quickly revised its plans. A world recession had kept commodity prices
down, and there seemed to be no upturn in the foreseeable future. In

the absence of any other natural resources that could be used to generate income, tourism, though much disliked by NJM planners and most other parties in the region, was the only pragmatic alternative, and a new airport was necessary if the island was going to be a serious contender for large numbers of tourists.

The existing airport, Pearls, was opened to traffic in January 1943 and was extended in 1948, but had become obsolete a decade later with the development of larger aircraft. In January 1955 the British firm of Scott, Wilson, Kirkpatrick and Partners recommended in a report on "Airfields for Grenada and St. Vincent" the development of the Point Salines site as being better able to handle the newer aircraft. At first mention of the new site there were some domestic objections. The taxi drivers' union objected because they claimed that the site would be so close to the hotels occupied by tourists that it would severely curtail their business. A subsequent report by a government agency again recommended Point Salines as a logical choice for a new airport and urged that "construction be started as soon as conveniently possible," as did a 1967 report by a tripartite commission of the United Kingdom, the United States, and Canada. The report recommended that development take place in stages so as to limit the burden of the cost involved.

By this time it was obvious to both the government and the people of Grenada that their economic well-being was being hurt by the absence of an international airport. The taxi drivers' union dropped its objections to the airport, and the government began to seek aid for its construction. Other sister Caribbean islands like Barbados and Antigua, which did not have to construct new airports but simply to lengthen their runways and improve their facilities, leaped past Grenada. They attracted new hotels and cashed in on the heavy influx of tourists from North America and Europe during the relatively prosperous sixties and early seventies. Grenada—lush, green, and picturesque, with white sandy beaches as good as or better than those of any other Caribbean island—languished. As more Grenadians began to travel, they found that they had become victims of the new advances in aviation. In order to get to North America or Europe, they had to catch connecting flights in Barbados or Trinidad; if there was a delay in either of their flights, they had to stay overnight on one of those two islands.

As the need for quick modern transportation grew, the government felt pressured to do something about a new airport. In mid–1976 the Civil Aviation Authority of London proposed night flying into Grenada's

Pearls airport and St. Vincent's Amos Vale. The regional airline serving the area and the Airline Pilots' Association accepted the proposal for St. Vincent, but not for Grenada. They gave as their reason the unfavorable topography and the need to use a steep, curved approach for landing. The decision was a further blow to the government and the economy. In late 1976 the World Bank sent a mission specifically to look at the airport development project. The team concluded that the existing runway at Pearls acted and would continue to act as a "constraint on the development of air transport and tourism growth." It also recommended that further study be made of the Point Salines site to determine its "technical, economic and financial feasibility." No further studies were done.

The New Jewel Movement, taking over in March 1979, quickly put together a panel of Caribbean technical experts, including Cubans, to advise them on the matter of an airport. The team recommended that work proceed at the Point Salines site, and construction began in January 1980. The plan called for a two-phase construction, the first being 7,800 feet, increasing to 9,000 feet when demand warranted it. By mid–1980, however, international airlines began replacing their B–707 aircraft with wide-bodied B–747s, DC–10s, and L–1011s. Since these larger craft began flying the Caribbean route into St. Lucia, Antigua, and Barbados, the Bishop government decided to construct the full-length airport straightaway.[4] Estimated cost was put at U.S. $70.9 million, a steep increase over the first proposal.

While preliminary work was underway, other related studies were being prepared. In August 1980 Messrs. Interinco International of Canada projected the number of people that would flow through the airport as follows:

1985	224,200
1990	334,400
1995	448,400
2000	547,200

In March 1981 the European Economic Community (EEC) Consultancy Report by Messrs. Sofreavia of Paris found that the estimates for installations and works to be undertaken were in order and did not consider any aspect of the project "too luxurious." Because the project had been so well documented, and because an international airport is such a basic part of a country's life today, the project was given a sympathetic ear by many Western governments.

But it was not simply for modern convenience that the airport had become necessary. The government saw it as "the most important project in Grenada's history." By this time the evidence of the benefits of an international airport had become much more evident. St. Lucia, a sister Caribbean island, opened its international airport in 1972. The benefits from tourism were immediately obvious.

Stay-Over Visitors[5]

	1970	1972	1973	1978	1980
Grenada	30,426	37,933	33,490	32,336	29,434
St. Lucia	29,529	42,399	45,809	69,300	85,000(est)

The Bishop government had seen the airport project as an investment that would get the tourism sector of the economy on its feet, encourage foreign investment in hotels, entice a greater number of tourists, and breathe new life into several aspects of other industries that also serve tourists. They also saw it as aiding their agricultural exports, which still had to be transhipped through Barbados and Trinidad.

Among people in the Caribbean, the development of Grenada's airport seemed no cause for alarm. Those who had visited the island knew of its natural beauty and tourist potential. It also did not take a trained aviation expert to see that the Pearls airport was inadequate and dangerous. The government was succeeding in a vitally important project, and if the Cuban government was among those assisting in a major way, it seemed to bother no one. Indeed, some of the biggest supporters of the project were the Chamber of Commerce, the Hotel Association, and many other groups that did not necessarily support the NJM government politically.

The Cuban connection was, however, noted by some Caribbean scholars. For some time academics in the region had argued privately that the Caribbean was treated with indifference by the United States because Caribbean leaders, by refusing to explore opportunities with the Soviet bloc or with any other source willing to finance and develop projects in the area, posed no threat to U.S. strategic interests. While they had privately criticized Castro's aid in Jamaica as "heavy-handed," they were quick to point out that he had given that island tangible help that other Western powers had not. Castro's involvement in the much-needed Grenada airport was considered a display of "willingness to help from a state that is not itself rich financially but has a well-trained work force."[6]

The Bishop government was much admired for its ingenuity in arranging the project. Bishop's use of socialist professionals from a number of islands in a consultative capacity gave him greater influence among writers and opinion molders. Little wonder, then, that U.S. reactions to Cuban involvement in building the airport were largely dismissed as resentment that a poor and neglected island within its hemisphere had moved on its own rather than waiting until the United States was ready and had played the superpower game to its own advantage.

It was the U.S. intelligence community that first became alarmed by the Cuban involvement in the construction of the airport. The Carter administration was at the time beleaguered by the Iranian hostage crisis and, facing an election, was not willing to make it an issue. However, the more conservative technocrats who formulate policy, and who fill the political appointments every president must make, were. The argument was that the airport under construction was a secret military airport for use by Cuba in its role as Soviet surrogate in Africa and the Middle East. It was supposedly being developed as a needed layover and refueling point.

The argument seems superficially plausible in the light of Castro's foray into Africa. One would not doubt that, having helped in the construction of an airport, the Cuban government would have assumed it available in a time of need, especially with a friendly government in control. However, the airport as it was being constructed had no military features. If international press reports that the Cubans had put 20,000 troops in Africa without a Grenada airport were true, why would they be spending $30 million for one this late in the game? Furthermore, why would the Bishop government have gone first to every West European government seeking aid?

But the concerns of the U.S. intelligence community and conservative technocrats were given scant attention under the Carter administration. On April 16, 1979, the State Department released a statement to the press to the effect that the United States had told Grenada that it would view with concern the establishment of close ties with Cuba.[7] On that same day Grenada announced that it had established diplomatic relations with Cuba.[8] Later in the month Grenada accepted and approved the proposal for a new U.S. ambassador, Sally Shelton. On May 9 Prime Minister Bishop, in a radio broadcast to the people of Grenada, said that he had received information from a high-level source that the Central Intelligence Agency had drawn up a plan to destabilize the government of Grenada. He outlined the three stages of the plan: "The plan was drawn up in the shape of a pyramid; at the bottom of the pyramid was a plan to destabilize the country by planting false reports about Grenada in newspapers, and on radio stations, also by encouraging prominent individuals, Organizations and Governments in the region to attack our Revolution.

"This first half of the plan was aimed at creating dissatisfaction and unrest among our people and also at wrecking our tourist industry and economy."

The second level of the pyramid "involves the use of violence and arson in the country," and if neither of these two methods succeeded in destabilizing the country, then the plan was to move to the stage of assassinating the leadership of the country, he added.[9]

Bishop said that it had become clear that the plan was already in operation and urged Grenadians to "make sure that these tactics of destabalization do not succeed." He pointed to two recent fires of suspicious origin as evidence that the plan had already become operational. But Bishop was well aware that the suspicious fires were possibly the work of a small group that had already become disaffected with his party because of the sharp leftist ideological turn the leadership had taken.

When on January 5, 1980, the government of Grenada proposed to the U.S. State Department that Ms. Dessima Williams be accredited as Grenada's ambassador to Washington, not even a reply was received, although the new U.S. ambassador, Sally Shelton, had travelled freely to Grenada and was treated with cordiality and respect by the government. If the government of Grenada was under any illusion about how far President Carter was prepared to go, it soon got an answer. In January Hurricane Allen devastated the agriculture of Grenada, St. Vincent and the Grenadines, St. Lucia, and Dominica. The Windward Islands Banana Association, the association representing all four islands, applied to the United States for assistance to rehabilitate the banana industries. The aid was granted, but with the stipulation that Grenada not be one of the recipients.

The islands unanimously rejected the aid rather than exclude Grenada. This condition attached by the Carter administration to desperately needed funds for the rehabilitation after a natural disaster demonstrated clearly the extent to which the U.S. administration was prepared to penalize the government of Grenada. In addition, Ambassador Shelton, after making two visits to Grenada from her residence in Barbados, was ordered not to have any further contact with the government. In June 1980 a bomb went off at a major NJM rally at Queens Park. The explosion killed three young women and injured many other people. The event convinced the government that the United States, through the CIA, was actively seeking to undermine it, though no evidence was ever found to substantiate this charge. The top party leaders were suspicious that the CIA or some such agency had formed an alliance with those former top members of the NJM who had left for ideological reasons and had enabled them to carry out these acts. This suspicion led to the first wave of arbitrary political arrests.

With the election of Ronald Reagan to the presidency, Grenada desperately hoped for an improvement in Grenada-U.S. relations. Its telegram of congratulations to the president-elect suggested some hope for a new beginning, as Reagan replied that he looked forward to "a mutual effort to promote friendly relations between our two nations."[10] But in choosing the technocrats for his administration, Mr. Reagan drew a substantial number of his personnel from the American Enterprise Institute, many of whose members had earlier publicly expressed alarm at Grenada's closeness with Cuba. As a result, when President Reagan entered office, rather than revising U.S. policy, he allowed the situation to continue to deteriorate with a greater intensity.

Grenada again submitted a proposal that an ambassador be accredited, and this time nominated Jimmy Emmanuel, a career diplomat. Again it received no answer or acknowledgement. In March 1981, after the government of Grenada had successfully negotiated a three-year loan of $6.3 million with the International Monetary Fund to assist in implementing its development program, the U.S. executive director of the IMF asked for an indefinite postponement of the request. The U.S. government also tried to discourage European governments from attending a previously arranged aid donors conference in Brussels to solicit funds for the construction of Grenada's international airport.

Such action by the U.S. government to discipline Grenada did not go unnoticed in the Caribbean. Rather, these attempts at economic sabotage brought Grenada sympathy, even from some of its critics. One of the more sympathetic and influential Caribbean papers viewed U.S. government policy toward Grenada as displaying some of the worst features of a superpower. While it expressed concern over the Grenadian government's unwillingness to set a date for elections or to bring political prisoners to trial, it argued that the Caribbean governments should not tolerate the hypocrisy of a Reagan White House that engaged in economic aggression against Grenada while carrying on business as usual in South Africa.[11]

The failure of the NJM to hold elections was a sore point for NJM supporters and admirers throughout the Caribbean. Many saw this as a failure to carry out an important promise. It was an issue over which the Bishop government and its friends expended a great deal of energy and one that kept the government on the defensive for much of its tenure in office. It is clear that even the Bishop government's most fervent supporters did not support its excesses, particularly its detention of political prisoners and the NJM's failure to hold elections. But many defended its right to maintain relations with whatever country it chose.

By hounding the government of Grenada, the United States lost credibility with friendly Caribbean governments and European allies, who did not see Grenada or the construction of an airport as undermining the strategic interests of the United States. For many years Caribbean and other Third World academics had argued that the U.S. government used political considerations in disapproving loans to countries whose governments pursued policies it did not like. But U.S. politicians, journalists, and scholars vigorously denied this assertion, and it was impossible for Caribbean and Third World academics to produce hard evidence to corroborate their charge. Now, twenty years later, the evidence was beginning to surface that showed precisely how the United States used its power. The directors of the Caribbean Development Bank, responsible for the channeling of aid to member governments, were approached by the U.S. government seeking support in its policy of exclusion against Grenada.[12] Not only did this act discredit the story that U.S. sources, both official and unofficial, had constantly given, but it also showed them to be either naive or hypocritical. This kind of reputation abroad has helped undermine the support that once reinforced U.S. foreign policy at home and has made that policy a much more contentious issue.

While the U.S. government was doing its best to undermine the government of Grenada, developments on the island itself were bringing admiration from its sympathizers. On January 29, 1981, Deputy Prime Minister and Minister of Planning, Finance, and Trade Bernard Coard began a unique exercise in economic planning. He assembled some 1,000 Grenadians for a National Conference of Delegates of Mass Organizations on the Economy. The delegates were to begin discussions on a comprehensive report on the national economy for 1981 and the prospects for 1982. The conference, it was claimed, was designed to promote popular participation in the formulation of the budget. The conference was preceded by discussions between Coard and members of the business community on how they could best contribute to the country's economic growth. Represented at the conference were delegates from all ten trade unions, the National Women's Organization, the National Youth Organization, the armed forces, and a number of smaller groups. Apart from the announced intentions of the conference, it was Coard's attempt to establish an identity of his own. Though not an overt move, this was his first attempt to infiltrate the party machinery for his own use later on.

Other more useful economic developments were also being undertaken. The establishment of the National Fisheries Corporation in April 1981 was hailed as a major achievement by the government. The new corporation began functioning with a fleet of seven vessels, six of them gifts from Cuba. Until then, Grenada had imported most of its preserved fish from Canada and Western Europe, supplemented by fresh fish from coastal fishing. The United States continued to resent the much-needed economic aid Grenada received from Cuba. In August the U.S. Navy began a series of large naval maneuvers in the Caribbean. Dubbed "Ocean Venture 81," they included a mock invasion of an island off Puerto Rico fictionally named Amber and the Amberdines. The Bishop government, feeling threatened by these exercises, put even greater stress on building an army and other paramilitary units to try to counter an invasion attempt. To stem the flood of negative reports, many of which Grenada felt were being planted from Washington, it hired a

New York public relations firm to help improve the island's image in the United States, its chief source of tourist revenue.

On his Easter vacation to Barbados in April 1982, President Reagan made a short stop in Jamaica to visit Prime Minister Seaga. The Reagan administration had formed close ties with the Seaga government because the two shared similar views on economics and politics. The Reagan administration had, as a result of their friendship, found novel ways to help the government of Jamaica through its economic crisis. In his speeches Mr. Seaga praised the president's Caribbean Basin Initiative, saying that the plan created "a new window of opportunity for hard-pressed Caribbean countries to create new employment and improved standards of living which are essential to all democratic systems of government."[13] But Prime Minister Seaga was especially grateful for the personal help Jamaica had received from the Reagan administration and thanked him especially for the purchase of 1.6 million tons of bauxite for the U.S. strategic reserve. This, Prime Minister Seaga said, amounted to "very critical support at the right time enabling us to weather the most difficult periods of our recovery."[14]

When he arrived in Barbados, President Reagan again sounded the anti-Cuban and anticommunist rhetoric that he had voiced in Jamaica. While he was in Barbados, the president conferred with five other leaders from the Caribbean area: Mr. J. G. M. Adams of Barbados, Mr. Milton Cato of St. Vincent and the Grenadines, Mr. Kennedy Simmonds of St. Kitts-Nevis, Mrs. Eugenia Charles of Dominica, and Mr. Vere Bird of Antigua and Barbuda. He expressed his concern that "Grenada had joined with the Soviet Union, Nicaragua and Cuba to 'spread the virus' of Marxism in the region."[15] But the Caribbean leaders were more concerned about their own economic position and argued that the $60 million they were to receive together under his Caribbean Basin Plan was insufficient.

In a televised speech to the nation in March 1983, Reagan launched a strong attack against Grenada with special emphasis on the construction of its international airport.[16] With reconnaissance photos he showed the construction of the airport, implying that it was a clandestine matter. The newspapers gave full coverage to the assertions, but did little to verify what the true situation actually was.

Time magazine attempted to do so and was able without hindrance to provide pictures of the airport under construction, including pictures of Cubans at work. Indeed, so popular was the construction of the airport that Prime Minister Bishop boasted: "The one mistake Reagan made was to interfere with the one project he should never touch." *Time*'s reporter found that neighboring islands were envious of the economic gifts Grenada had received as a result of its Cuban alliance while they were still waiting for their "promised share of the U.S. Caribbean Basin Initiative," held up by Congress in a fight with the Reagan administration over its total Latin American policy. The reporter also found that U.S. opposition to Bishop had increased his popularity in the Caribbean and within Grenada itself. "Some of the government's highest marks, in fact, come from its chief critics," one such critic noted. "I would vote for them if they trusted us with a free vote but they won't, so I am one of their attackers." On the whole, the reporter found that Grenadians were generally satisfied with their government. He was impressed with the hard work of its political leadership and still more with the economic development they were pursuing. On the question of the airport he reported: "None of the revolution's accomplishments is greater than the $70 million international airport due for completion next year. It may seem extravagant and dangerous to Washington, which fears that Soviet or Cuban military aircraft may want to use the nearly two-mile-long strip, but if free elections were held the government of Prime Minister Bishop would win hands down on just this issue."[17]

Although few papers and news magazines followed up on the president's assertion, even fewer bothered to investigate the financial and physical aspects of the airport. Had they done so, they would have found that a U.S. firm, Layne Dredging of Miami, had dredged the inlet across which the runway extends, and that Plessey, a British company, had contracted to install a navigational and communications system.[18] They would have found also that the airport had absolutely no military features at all. Most importantly, they would have found that there was nothing at all extraordinary about the length of the airport, as most Caribbean airports are about the same size.

Country	Runway Length
Antigua	9,000 feet
Aruba	8,997 feet
Bahamas	11,000 feet

Country	Runway Length
Barbados	11,000 feet
Curaçao	11,187 feet
Dominican Republic	11,000 feet
Guadeloupe	11,499 feet
Jamaica	8,565 feet
Martinique	10,827 feet
Puerto Rico	10,002 feet
St. Lucia	9,000 feet
Trinidad	9,500 feet
Venezuela	11,483 feet
Grenada	5,250 feet (present)
	9,000 feet (proposed)

March 1983 was filled with good economic news for Grenada. Opening ceremonies were held for completion of a new telephone exchange for the capital, St. George's, the first part of a new system being installed by East Germany through a soft loan. A few days after his televised address President Reagan returned to the subject in a speech to the National Association of Manufacturers. He again asserted, "It is not nutmeg that is at stake in the Caribbean and Central America, it is the United States' national security." To show its defiance, the government of Grenada made a special effort to get the public to attend what ended up as a larger-than-usual rally on March 12 to thank Cuba for a cement-block factory it had constructed. The plant, named for the Nicaraguan revolutionary Augusto Sandino, was intended to produce material for the construction of the airport and to manufacture prefabricated housing units.[19] In his keynote address at the opening of the plant, Deputy Prime Minister Coard denounced the U.S. government.

In a country with only twenty thousand families, a housing plant that can produce five hundred homes a year is a giant step forward. In a fairly short space of time, this country will be able to wipe out its housing problem. And for this we must thank the government and people of Cuba.

What Reagan and his cowboys really fear Cuba for is not their military aid but their economic assistance. They are frightened by twenty-five doctors training in Cuba. They are afraid the masses of an English-speaking Caribbean society will ask, "If Grenada could build five hundred housing units a year, why can't we?" . . . they are afraid that Grenada is being held up as a model for the developing world.

Prime Minister Bishop saw what he called "this latest threat from Ronald Reagan" in more political terms. He said that it "means a throwing down of the gauntlet to our revolution. He is clearly signaling that they are getting ready for an all-out assault against our revolutionary process. . . . They are now sitting down and planning the final stages of armed attack against our revolution. But we are not going to be threatened or intimidated. They can drop a bomb and wipe our country off the face of the earth, but if they come to try and invade, when they land, they will discover the fighting will of the Grenadian people. We will never give up." What was left unsaid was that many of the new projects begun by the NJM government were only modestly successful. While they contributed to the infrastructure and even at times moved the economy in new directions, they were a financial drain on the unfulfilled government. As a result, the government had to seek more aid to make up the difference. Politically, at home people were becoming disenchanted with the promises of the revolution. They knew of the shortcomings of the economic projects, disliked the sacrifices they were constantly being urged to make, and were tired of the political rallies and rhetoric. In the Caribbean area and further afield, however, the economic changes and many of the political positions of the government were applauded by admirers of the government.

While the public posture of high NJM government officials was to take the political offensive, they were privately worried, especially those who made up the moderate wing of the party. They had always wanted good relations with the United States and saw the opportunity drifting further and further away. It was this feeling that prompted Prime Minister Bishop once again to request the appointment of an ambassador of Grenada to the United States; once again, there was no reply.

Grenada's economic development was having an effect among the smaller islands of the Caribbean. In an interview in April 1983 the foreign minister of Barbados, Mr. Lewis Tull, while expressing the concern many had for security within the area, was more concerned about the fact that Grenada had received over $23 million in aid in 1982 from a number of Eastern and Western sources. In fact, one diplomat called Grenada "the most lavishly aided island in the region."[20] Mr. Reagan's rhetoric seems to have convinced Mr. Tull and presumably other Caribbean officials that "most of Washington's concern revolves around U.S.-Soviet strategic competition that has little to do with the island's economic problems".[21] While expressing some admiration for what Bishop was trying to accomplish in Grenada, the foreign minister saw the position of the Reagan administration as "extreme." Tull put it this way: "We cannot resolve it with the more extreme position that the United States might be disposed to take. I don't expect the government of Grenada to back off. They've gone too far. You have to live with them." Mr. Tull said that Maurice Bishop had given the Caricom heads of government a "solemn undertaking" to institute a system that would lead to genuine democracy and eventual elections. While noting that several islands were "very concerned about security matters," more so than they had been for years, he went on to emphasize that they were more concerned "about welfare, about education, about housing." He then stated in blunt terms his impatience with U.S. economic policy toward the area. "It does create a feeling of disillusionment among the micro Caribbean states that pinned their faith on U.S. aid when they find they are getting relatively—I want to be fair—relatively less aid than Cuba or Grenada."[22]

While the government of Grenada had pursued a radical foreign policy, its domestic economic policy was very pragmatic. Shortly after assuming power, the government had notions of giving up tourism altogether, but this idea was dropped quickly when Hurricane Allen destroyed much of the banana crop and when nutmeg prices tumbled not long after. The government then became committed to diversification, according to chief economic planner Clairmont Kirton. "No displacement of the private sector is taking place."[23] Faced with a 30 percent drop in tourism, Grenada paid for forty travel writers to visit the island and make their own assessment of the situation for their audience, first eliminating many of the tedious checks the government had imposed during the first months of the revolution. This approach to economic development culminated in a law offering incentives for new investments in Grenada's economy.

Still, Bishop and his government needed to have good relations with the United States. As a result, he made an impromptu trip to Washington in June 1983 to try to do some fence mending. In Washington he met with National Security Adviser William Clark and a few low-level diplomats at the State Department. Neither President Reagan nor Secretary of State Shultz would see him. The Reagan administration was in no mood to embrace Bishop, despite his efforts at conciliation. The message he received was the same: good relations with the United States could only come when he distanced himself from Cuba. Bishop had taken a personal risk in making the trip, for the left wing of his party had argued against any such attempt. His failure convinced them and others within his party that the United States had no intention of resuming good relations until the NJM government was out of office. In August 1982 Grenada finally obtained its loan from the International Monetary Fund despite the objections of the United States government. It was a personal triumph for Finance Minister Coard, who had worked tirelessly against great odds to get the loan. Within a few weeks the euphoria that accompanied this success would end.

NOTES

1. Michael Massing, "Grenada Before and After," *Atlantic Monthly*, February 1984, p. 80.

2. Ibid., p. 81.

3. As quoted in Anthony P. Maingot, "Options for Grenada," *Caribbean Review* 12, no. 4, (Fall 1983): 26.

4. In this section I have relied heavily on Bernard Coard, Minister of Finance, Opening Address to Aid Donors Conference, International Airport Project, Brussels, April 14–15, 1981.

5. Ibid.

6. Discussion with University of the West Indies Professor (St. Augustin).

7. *New York Times*, April 17, 1979, p. A5.

8. Ibid.

9. Caribbean News Agency, Barbados, May 9, 1979. OAS Daily Bulletin Servicio Informatiyo, May 10, 1979.

10. Letters to President Reagan by Maurice Bishop, reprinted in *Caribbean Contact*, March 1982.

11. *Caribbean Contact*, July 1981.

12. Edward Cody, "Grenada Unsettles Its Neighbors, But So Does U.S. Reaction," *Washington Post*, April 24, 1983, p. A34.

13. Adam Clymer, "Jamaica's Premier Praised by Reagan," *New York Times*, April 8, 1982.

14. Ibid.

15. Steven R. Weisman, "Reagan in Caribbean, Links Grenada to Moscow," *New York Times*, April 9, 1982.

16. Ronald Reagan, televised speech to the nation, March 23, 1983.

17. William McWhirter, *Time*, May 2, 1983.

18. Massing, "Grenada Before and After," p. 82.

19. Ibid., p. 83.

20. Cody, "Grenada Unsettles Its Neighbors," p. A34.

21. Lewis Tull, as quoted by Cody, "Grenada Unsettles Its Neighbors," p. A34.

22. Ibid.

23. Barbara Crossette, "Grenada Looks to Cuban Ways and U.S. Tourists," *New York Times*, February 7, 1982.

3

Revolution and Reaction

One of the most difficult problems confronting opposition groups is how to proceed against an incumbent government, which has not only the power of legitimacy, but also the security apparatus of the state to insure that it stays in power. The seizure of power by Maurice Bishop and the NJM was a bloodless coup d'état. Their effort to label it a revolution was an attempt to give their illegal seizure a legitimacy that they themselves knew it lacked. That Bishop's finance minister, Bernard Coard, should try the same method four years later as he attempted to supplant Bishop as prime minister should have come as no surprise. But coups always are a surprise, and worst of all, once the fever is contracted, it is very contagious, making close neighbors extremely uneasy.

The Bishop-NJM coup of 1979 produced a number of aftershocks that made many people concerned for the stability of the whole Caribbean area. Early in 1980, just after the St. Vincent Labour party (headed by Milton Cato) was declared the winner in the national elections, rioting broke out on Union Island, one of the smaller islands of St. Vincent and the Grenadines. A group led by a little-known politician claimed that the elections were rigged and fomented disturbances. Cato, a veteran political leader who had been in and out of office several times, appealed to the prime minister of Barbados for assistance, and he in turn sent in the Barbados Regiment to put down the riot. Shortly after, on the island of St. Lucia a political crisis was precipitated when Deputy Prime Minister George Odlum tried to take control of the government. In the war of words that followed, prime minister Allan Louisy accused his deputy of having sent St. Lucians to Grenada for military training without his approval or knowledge. So bitter and divisive was the leadership struggle that they split their party, allowing an opposition parliamentary maneuver that forced the governor to call new elections. The subsequent election of veteran politician John Compton as prime minister brought the crisis to an end.[1]

The most bizarre of the disturbances occurred in Dominica. There were attempts to seize power in April 1981 by a group that had penetrated the police force, hoping to use it in the takeover. One secret police officer was killed in the attempt. The establishment of a link between the leaders of the attempted takeover and the Ku Klux Klan in New Orleans presented an ironic and troubling twist to the episode. Shortly thereafter, the Prime Minister of Dominica disbanded the defense force.

As always in these islands, the clashes were between the old established political parties and new political groups impatient to assume office. That most of these groups had to form their own political vehicle to promote an alternative to both the governing and the official opposition parties indicates the extent to which the leaders of the established parties create problems for themselves by giving the impression that young people have limited opportunity for political expression and development.

Democracy, as it confronts many of the young persons waiting in the wings, is not as most imagine it to be. Because the rhetoric of youth tends to be harsh and strident, and because it proposes solutions that often break with the past, young newcomers are quickly branded as radicals and treated severely for their views. There is a great difference between growing up politically in a culture that entertains and discusses different ideas and in one in which political leaders act in an authoritarian manner. One veteran observer seeing this attitude at work took a more sympathetic view of what one specific group, the anti–nuclear war movement in Europe, was trying to accomplish. His assessment could apply to most newly founded movements: "Like any great spontaneous popular movement, this one has, and must continue to have, its ragged edges, and even its dangers. It will attract the freaks and the extremists. Many of the wrong people will attach themselves to it. It will wander off in mistaken directions and become confused with other causes that are less worthy. It already shows need of leadership and centralized organization."[2]

In the Commonwealth Caribbean many of the parties are patterned after the British Labour party. At the time these parties were founded, their leaders had the sympathy of members of Parliament in Britain, of congressmen in the United States, and of the trade unions on both sides of the Atlantic. Even though the Caribbean was carrying on a domestic fight against a colonial power, some sort of dialogue did exist between the leaders and those within the establishment who were at least willing to talk. For the present generation of leaders, induction into politics has been quite different and begins most often at the local U.S embassy when they are applying for entry to the United States. Here, because of their political affiliation and rhetoric, they are questioned, examined, and interrogated, and very often in the end refused an entrance visa to the United States under the McCarran-Walter Act.[3]

In most cases this rejection for visiting the world's most highly proclaimed democracy is a devastating blow, not because they are denied something, but because they have hope in the system and want to have their ideas challenged and discussed; their opinions are not yet fully formed and are ready to be modified and changed after discussion. A visa is a chance for the United States to influence young leaders, a chance the United States discards by excluding opinion leaders.

In exasperation some responsible Americans often suggest that these people should take their rhetoric to Moscow where it would be appreciated. To say this is to miss the point. Many of these people have the chance to attend conferences and meetings in the Soviet bloc countries; some attend, but most are not so willing.

Given this situation, Caribbean and other Third World leaders must themselves make the kind of gestures necessary for accommodating and training the new generations of leaders at home. The risks are too great to do otherwise. The apparent willingness by Third World modernizers to be part of a progressive scene is not recognized and encouraged by many policymakers in the West. Rather, the young leaders are easily lumped together as either Communists or troublemakers and simply dismissed. With no model abroad to examine and emulate, the only path left is a fierce ideological struggle at home. It is against this psychological background that events in Grenada unfolded in October 1983.

The stunning news of Bishop's overthrow shocked many and confirmed the worst fears of others in the Caribbean. First news of the coup was picked up in the Caribbean on Friday, October 14, 1983. At

that time it was learned merely that Maurice Bishop had been replaced
as the head of the government. Because of the way the Bishop government had come to power, because of the disturbances that followed
in surrounding islands, and because of Grenada's strong friendship with
Cuba and the Reagan administration's pointed objection to this, there
was a great deal of Caribbean interest in Grenada's domestic affairs.
Immediately upon receiving the news of the coup, neighboring leaders
asked, Where is Maurice Bishop? It eventually leaked out that Bishop
had been placed under house arrest. This bit of news, as the leaders of
the coup had quite rightly anticipated, triggered a chain of reactions
domestically and internationally.

The coup set two new precedents. A politician, with the cooperation
of the army, could usurp power; and a politician and head of government, once ousted from office, could be put under house arrest. Grenada's neighbors were understandably uncomfortable about this. The
prime minister of Barbados, in a speech to his nation, summed up the
attitude of his government this way: "I considered that the house arrest
of a Prime Minister was an act so extreme as to imply some measure
of imminent violence and disorder."[4] On that day he conveyed his fears
to the foreign minister of Grenada, Mr. Unison Whiteman, after learning
that he was in transit to Grenada at the Barbados International Airport.
He suggested that Mr. Whiteman not return home and offered him
political asylum in Barbados.[5] The Grenadian foreign minister refused
his offer and returned home.

As Mr. Adams had predicted, domestic turmoil began that Saturday,
October 15. This threat of turmoil and anarchy that could possibly spread
to the other islands, given their high rates of unemployment and the
depressed state of their economies, worried politicians in the islands
situated close to Grenada. By this time Adams had already concluded
that "whatever our differences in the past, Mr. Bishop deserved the
support of Caribbean governments in the circumstances, and sought
opinion on whether he could be got out of the hands of his enemies
and the situation given an opportunity to stabilize." Interestingly
enough, Adams was not the only one who considered a rescue mission
at this early date. A member of his Department of Defense and Security
was approached on Saturday by a U.S. official about the possibility of
a rescue mission for Bishop and with an offer to transport him out of
Grenada.[6] After he spoke to other prime ministers in the area, however,
his enthusiasm quickly waned. As Adams saw it, the only questions

were whether the new regime would allow Bishop to leave, and whether Bishop himself wished to leave. But Prime Minister Cato of St. Vincent and the Grenadines strongly questioned the plan. Cato argued that "it would clearly not have been right to attempt to save Bishop, and to ignore the detainees, some of whom had spent more than four years behind bars" under the Bishop government.[7] News filtered out from Grenada of a continuously deteriorating political situation. At a meeting of the Barbados cabinet on October 19 it was agreed to proceed with the rescue plan "in collaboration with the Eastern Caribbean countries and larger non-Caribbean countries with the resources necessary to carry out such an intricate operation." But events in Grenada preempted the decision even as it was being made. Bishop and several of his ministers were killed.

Maurice Bishop had been in a precarious position for some time. He and his government had managed, despite early crises, to convince many people by their hard work and efficiency that they truly had nothing but the welfare of their country at heart. Some people were convinced, others were not. Those who were not and who made an attempt to express their feelings were dealt with harshly. Many were put in prison without trial.

But it was in external relations that Bishop found his stiffest challenge. Adverse publicity drastically reduced Grenada's tourist trade, a market that had already suffered badly because of the world recession. The sagging economy gave the left wing of the party greater confidence to call for radical changes, the very opposite of what U.S. policy hoped to accomplish. Within the Caribbean region, too, Bishop was under pressure from a number of his colleagues to free some of his political prisoners and hold elections. In his attempt to respond to these pressures, he ran afoul of his own party's left wing. In the end it was a naked struggle for power that finally brought him down. Because no one person or group of persons came forward soon enough to give any explanation as to how and why Bishop and his colleagues were killed, many believed that law and order had broken down and that another power struggle was taking place, possibly among the NJM civilian leaders and the army. This allowed rumors to run wild in the region and contributed to a deepening sense of pessimism for the outcome.

According to the first secretary of the Grenadian embassy in Cuba, events leading to Bishop's downfall began approximately a month earlier. The New Jewel Movement's Central Committee held a secret meeting from September 14 to 16, 1983, "to analyze the state of the revolution—it had reached a point of stagnation."[8] In reality, the moderate wing of the party had in its years of dominance been unable to convince many Western countries and institutions that what it cared about most was the development of its country. The left wing of the party, seeing no progress in this area, was maneuvering in an attempt to take control. The internal struggle had gone on for some time; now, after a series of moves within the party and the government, this group was ready to take charge.

On the first day of the meeting the committee voted nine to one with three abstentions to have Bishop continue as head of state, but splitting his responsibility so as to have Bernard Coard assume control of the economy and party matters. The meeting reached a consensus that "certain members had too many responsibilities, and as a result all of their responsibilities were suffering." This new arrangement, it was thought, was the best way to take advantage of the talents of both men. As they saw it, Bishop "has always been very good in the international world and very popular with the masses, while Coard was very strong in the economic aspect of the revolution." The new arrangement "was to be an internal matter, a party question, and not to be publicized." The three who abstained included General Hudson Austin, who had missed most of the debate because he was abroad; Unison Whiteman, who claimed not to be sure about the arrangement; and Bishop himself, who said he needed time to think. He claimed that the idea was a "good one," but he had "practical reservations." Since the decision was binding, Bishop asked the meeting for time to think about the way in which such an arrangement would work.[9]

It was known that Deputy Prime Minister Bernard Coard had harbored ambitions of becoming prime minister. He and a number of people within the party were not satisfied with concessions being demanded by other governments. The question of elections was one main obstacle. As long as the structure remained as it was then, Bishop was the nominal leader of the NJM. But were a constitution written and accepted, and elections held, he would be the undisputed leader in a new organizational arrangement. It would then be difficult for Coard to move against Bishop other than through procedural means. In the intervening period, Coard had gone out and organized a number of conferences embracing many political, economic, and cultural groups under the guise of seeking their input into the overall economic plans for the country, but at the same time building for himself the political base he had never had within the NJM. In addition, he had just prior to the crisis made a number of political moves within the party and government to boost his own position for the leadership of the party. Coard had engineered a small pay raise for the army and reorganized the structure of the party, making himself chairman of four of five of the party's executive committees, with Bishop chairing only one.[10] Further, he had seen to it that his clique had a majority on these committees.

On the other hand, Maurice Bishop spent so much time travelling on aid and political missions that he did not have time to devote to the building of a wider political base for the NJM. His constant travels were due to the fact that once the United States had objected to his politics, it was almost mandatory that he be present to persuade aid donors that this was mere overreaction by the United States. Preoccupied as the NJM was with showing itself to be competent in its economic development and financial planning, given the years of Gairy irresponsibility, Bishop left himself little time for thinking about anything else. In addition, he had come to rely heavily on Coard's administrative and political skills. Most of all he wanted unity in his small, diminishing party. The decision to split the leadership was an attempt by Coard and his friends to capitalize on Bishop's frequent absences and inattention to the development of the party, something most people within the party would have agreed to, not suspecting that Coard and his clique would have the nerve to grab ultimate leadership. Since Bishop had never been officially made leader of the NJM and was joint coordinating secretary of the early NJM, the idea of shared responsibility was acceptable, as it had worked well while the group was out of government. However, what the average party members failed to understand was that being in office changed the nature of the role of each party leader, and for some, ambition assumed a position greater than their cause.

Despite the passage of this critical resolution, Bishop, though worried, did not do much about it. Rather, he began making preparations for a scheduled trip to Eastern Europe. On the eve of his departure, September 27, 1983, another party meeting was held at which Bishop accepted the resolution proposing "joint leadership." Four days after he arrived back home, October 12, a rumor hit the streets that Bernard Coard and his wife were trying to kill Bishop. Reaction to the rumor was so strong that the streets were almost empty; a party meeting was called for that evening. Upon investigation by the security forces, though, the rumor was traced to Bishop himself. His personal security guard said that Bishop had asked him to contact a number of opinion makers with the news. He called two of the people on the list before contacting the security forces about the matter. No matter what the truth is about this incident, it seems clear that Bishop felt the effects of an erosion of his power and a personal threat to his safety upon his return home.

At the meeting Bishop was asked to try to ease the tension. He went to the radio station, where he denied the rumor, but by this time most people knew that some important political development was afoot. The following day, October 13, another meeting was held to inform NJM Central Committee members about developments.

The meeting, however, seemed to take the form of a trial. The chief of national security read a sworn statement from Bishop's personal security guard stating that it was Bishop who had begun the rumors. Bishop made a forty-five–minute speech admitting that he had not carried out the instructions of the party, referring to the decision that he share his responsibilities with Coard. But while admitting culpability for that, he denied starting the rumor.[11] When he finished his speech, his security guard was again asked to address the meeting. He reiterated his accusations in detail, and Bishop was called upon to deny them. This he refused to do. "The general opinion there was that he was responsible for the rumor, due to his own failure to deny it."[12] Thereafter a number of proposals were adopted. The most important were the expulsion of Bishop from the party and placing him under house arrest. The main reason cited for house arrest was to prevent counterrevolutionaries from "aggravating the situation by making an attempt on his life."[13] But a more accurate reason for his confinement was that the small clique who had engineered his downfall knew that they had only the army behind them and could not risk having Bishop put his case to the people. The ensuing confrontation would have meant that the country would become involved in a political struggle, and control would slip from the hands of the clique.

One must admire the shrewd way in which Coard went about taking power away from a very popular leader. Rather than oppose Bishop openly, he did so through the executive arm of the party. By taking control of party affairs, he could control the activity and eventually the power base of Bishop himself. But it must have shocked Maurice Bishop that the Central Committee could have voted so consistently against him with so little apparent regard for the possible consequences to him personally and to the leadership of the party. Their reliance on ideology and form had become so complete that it had blinded even Bishop's friends to the intrigues and ambitions of some members of their group until it was too late.

What is even more fascinating is the apparently casual way he reacted to the first indications of his loss of support. Bishop had ignored many warnings from cabinet members about Coard's attempts to replace him. He assumed that his friends, all of whom had at times lived and worked together and had suffered under Eric Gairy together, would support him in a crunch, but the situation had changed drastically since they had entered office. The arrests of those opposed to the government and the lack of toleration for public criticism had taught people to be cautious in sharing their opinions, and when Coard began to use what was said freely in committee meetings to show noncommittee but influential party leaders that some people were not supporting the ideology of the party, they became even more cautious. Voting with the majority might have seemed the safest move. Arbitrary arrests and imprisonment generated an air of uncertainty, especially in such a small society as Grenada, where the modernizing elite and political activists are few and tend to know, or know of, each other.

Party executives felt further strain from the long meetings they were required to attend. This constant round of meetings, rallies, and trips abroad took a physical and an emotional toll. In addition, the ideological study groups that most executives and ranking members attended obscured their sense of realism. This bewildering rush of events created a need for some explanation for what was going on, and in the absence of any systematic party education, the language of the Revo, as the Grenadians referred to their revolution, was that of Marxism-Leninism. However, as one historian notes, "The curse of ideology is that it impoverishes our sense of reality; it impoverishes our imagination, too."[14]

It was in this milieu that Bishop chose to fly off to Europe and Cuba, after such a damning resolution had passed by a big majority. This suggests that Bishop had lost touch with what was going on in the party and illustrates how much he was preoccupied with obtaining economic and political support abroad. Constant electrical power failures in the city had made Bishop's trip absolutely critical. His mission was to persuade governments to assist Grenada economically. He succeeded in getting two generators from the Hungarians. His need for economic and political support was made more urgent by economic and political pressure from the United States, which was attempting to bring Grenada into line but succeeding only in fueling the left-wing argument within the party. The increase in unemployment, drop in investment, and lack of repair and maintenance of the infrastructure meant that either aid had to be found or the government would be seen as a failure.

The U.S. policy, unfortunately, did not take into account the pressures and party demands influencing Bishop. Even in a closed society, factional rivalries and ideological differences affect a leader's ability to control events while preserving his own position. It is ironic that Bishop, under house arrest, sought to make contact with the same opinion leaders he had as head of the government so easily put in prison.

Bishop's "Line of March" speech delivered on September 13, 1982, is the strongest piece of evidence most people use to show the seriousness of the NJM government and of Bishop himself in turning Grenada into a Communist state. Though the content of the speech and its thrust cannot be denied, this writer sees his growth and political development in a slightly different light. Many of those who knew Bishop personally doubted whether he had ever read Marx or any other Communist theoretician as a student or during his early years in politics. This writer seriously doubts whether he had the time and discipline to do so after he became a full-time politician. However, his early friendship with Fidel Castro and his rejection by the U.S. administration put him in a position of much greater importance than he or his small nation were accustomed to. The result was that he and other members of his party seemed to think that they had to act the part. They became more strident in their rhetoric and found their classification as radicals both romantic and convenient; they seemed to glory in being able to trade barbs with a superpower. Especially after they reneged on their promise to hold elections, they found their status a valuable guise behind which to hide their capricious arrests and imprisonment of opponents.

Putting Maurice Bishop under house arrest was the death knell of the NJM, its political experiment, and the clique that was attempting to usurp power. Holding him incommunicado allowed everyone to speculate as to his whereabouts and his safety. Many newspapers in the region demanded in bold headlines: Where is Bishop? The reaction domestically and throughout the Caribbean was so strong that it must have shocked even his captors. The failure of whoever was in charge to come forward and explain what was going on worried everyone and only intensified speculation. No one worried more than Grenada's neighbors in the Caribbean, who had for some time been keeping a watchful eye on developments there. Domestically the guarded nature of the earlier NJM meetings and the developing crisis added to the air of confusion.

The day after Bishop was placed under house arrest (October 14, 1983), National Mobilization Minister Selwyn Strachan announced that Bernard Coard had taken over as prime minister.[15] Because Strachan was known to be a close friend of Bernard Coard, credibility was given to the statement as the news was flashed around the Caribbean. However, by 3:30 P.M. the state-controlled radio announced the resignation of Bernard Coard as minister of finance. He claimed that he had resigned to make it abundantly clear that the rumor of his being out to assassinate Bishop was "a vicious lie." While Coard's resignation perplexed many and further added to the confusion, some saw it as a clever ploy to extricate himself from developments he did not anticipate and could not control. When Selwyn Strachan had made his announcement, a crowd had gathered quickly outside the office and demanded that Bishop continue in power. "No Bishop, no revolution," they shouted. Strong protests were also flooding Coard from fraternal organizations and individual friends throughout the Caribbean.

Strachan's announcement could have been premature and made without Coard's knowledge, or he could have been flying a kite to test the climate before Coard emerged. Whatever the case, Coard's resignation was a grievous tactical error. Having precipitated a political crisis, great revolutionaries step forward and take control to give the revolution direction and not allow the political situation to degenerate into anarchy. By resigning, Coard left no one in charge, allowing the situation to appear muddled and confused. By then he was in no position to control what anyone did, leaving less experienced operatives to perform delicate tasks in a highly charged atmosphere with which he would ultimately be linked. Even though Coard had resigned, the mood of the Caribbean clearly was against him and his role in the crisis. One newspaper headline mocked, "He Was Deputy and He Looked The Part."[16]

On the third day of the crisis nothing happened to make the situation any clearer to the people of either Grenada or the Caribbean. At about 11:00 A.M. the minister of fisheries and industrialization, Kendrick Radix, led a group of about 300 protesting Bishop's arrest from Market Square in central St. George's to the dock area on the eastern end of town, where he addressed them. He told them that he had been warning since last year that Coard intended to seize power. He urged them to demonstrate their support for Bishop and their rejection of Coard. "If Maurice is not released by Monday, there must be no work, no school and no play in Grenada."[17] He then told the group not to be surprised if many of them were imprisoned later that night, but added that he did not think that Coard would use the army against them. Despite his optimism, Radix was arrested later in the day for organizing and leading a demonstration. Later it was learned that he had also resigned from the government.

That evening Major Leon Cornwall, Grenada's ambassador to Cuba, read a statement on Radio Free Grenada reiterating the charges and accusations against Bishop. It was the first official acknowledgement of the crisis and for the first time placed the military in the middle of the dispute. Having an army officer read the statement was an attempt by Coard, the man behind the crisis and still in control of the party apparatus, to insert the army into the dispute, but it is possible that he hoped that its prominence would subdue a restive domestic population. By October 16, political analysts had concluded that should Bishop not retract the stand he had taken thus far of not negotiating with Coard or his representatives, Coard would be called upon to take over the party. A front-page editorial in one paper gave an indication of the frustration and fear that the crisis had generated in the Caribbean region as it continued, with special concern for the apparent involvement of the army and a Cuban presence. It further expressed sympathy for the people of Grenada, who did not know from one day to the next who might be running the country.[18]

On Monday, October 17, the gravity of the crisis intensified as the press, organizations, and individuals friendly to the NJM continued to bombard Coard and the NJM with telegrams and the Trinidad and Barbados press sought interviews by phone with anyone who could shed some light on what was truly going on. This prompted General Hudson Austin, Grenada's army commander, to make a statement over the radio.[19] He assured listeners that Maurice Bishop was at home and safe, then went on to give a detailed account of events leading to the crisis. He explained the crisis and the delay in informing citizens in the following manner:

We have never spoken about these problems publicly, because we thought it was vital to maintain an appearance of full unity of our party at all costs, especially concerning the attacks which the Grenada revolution has received from outside.

However, the truth is that during the past year, our party has faced a serious problem on the constantly growing desire of Comrade Maurice Bishop to exercise full and exclusive power and authority.[20]

The statement was the first full explanation of events that led to the crisis. But the fact that it came from the commander of the army was a great source of concern throughout the Caribbean. To have the army mixed up in a political party dispute left many people uneasy and frightened. However, confirmation that Bishop was safe and well was welcome news.

No sooner had people's fears begun to subside than, on the following day, Foreign Minister Unison Whiteman announced that five ministers, himself included, had resigned or expected to do so shortly. (The other four ministers were Lyden Ramdhanny, minister of tourism; Norris Bain, minister of housing; George Louison, minister of agriculture; and Jacqueline Creft, minister of education.) This was done to protest the decision made by the Central Committee to put Bishop under house arrest and to show that he still had the loyalty and support of most members of his cabinet. But it was a political maneuver that had come too late in the face of the ambition of a few determined people. It was interpreted by some Caribbean leaders as merely another sign that the domestic situation in Grenada was degenerating quickly and could end up as an all-out struggle between the majority civilian politicians on the one hand and a few leaders backed by the army on the other.

Coming on the heels of Bernard Coard's and Kendrick Radix's resignations, this meant that only three original members of Bishop's cabinet were still functioning: Christopher DeRiggs, minister of health; Army Commander Hudson Austin; and Minister of Construction and Information Selwyn Strachan. But in announcing the joint resignations, Unison Whiteman gave a few concrete details of events that were taking place in the background. "Comrade Coard, who is now running Grenada, has refused to engage in serious talks to resolve the crisis."[21] He reported that both he and George Louison had sought a meeting with Bernard Coard and his chief supporter within the cabinet, Selwyn Strachan, on October 15 to discuss the crisis. At the meeting, which took place on the following day, they advanced a set of compromise proposals for ending the crisis. These included a demand that Bishop remain prime minister, with the question of party leadership subject to later negoti-ation. This meant that Coard would share duties with Bishop in the party. The other provision was for Bishop to remain an executive mem-ber of the party until the leadership issue was resolved.

In response to these proposals, Coard complained that they did not go far enough and would require further meetings. It would appear that he wanted the leadership issue settled once and for all, and since he had the votes on the Central Committee, he was prepared to play the crisis to the end to force a decision favorable to himself. After that, no further personal meetings seemed to be desired. When George Louison attempted to carry on the discussions on the telephone, Coard terminated the conversation abruptly. Then, according to Whiteman, "It became clear to us that they did not want a settlement and seemed determined to use force and provoke violence, to achieve their objective."[22] But by this time Coard was assured of the backing of the army and probably did not see the need to negotiate for what he would eventually have anyway.

By Wednesday, October 19, the crisis had been going on for a week, and people were tired and frustrated that the situation had not been resolved. Their frustration gave way to action when Unison Whiteman, Vincent Noel, and others led a group of 10,000 people in a spontaneous act of self-assertion to the residence where Bishop was under house arrest. They defied the guards who fired warning shots, entered the residence, and forcibly freed Bishop. Bishop was clearly overcome by the spontaneous outpouring of emotion and personal risk for him as a leader. The action of the people reaffirmed his faith in himself and gave him the will to confront his adversaries. He and a number of his ministers set out with the crowd behind them to confront his enemies. As he walked through the streets of St. George's at the head of the procession, his supporters shouted, "We got our leader back."

But he had underestimated the resolve of his enemies to hold onto the power they had seized. The crowd, with Bishop and members of his cabinet in the lead, stormed Fort Rupert, the Armed Forces Head-quarters. The soldiers were ordered by Bishop not to shoot, and they surrendered their arms. According to the official reports, Bishop and his supporters set about arming themselves with these weapons. A detachment of soldiers was sent to reestablish control over the fort when the army commanders learned what had happened, and as they attempted to do so, Bishop and his supporters fired at them. The soldiers returned fire, and Maurice Bishop and five other top NJM members as well as a number of supporters were killed.[23]

This official version given by the Provisional Revolutionary Government of the tragedy differs from eyewitness accounts, which report that Bishop and his colleagues surrendered to the soldiers when the army stormed Fort Rupert and then were executed later.[24] The army commander, General Hudson Austin, immediately took charge, issuing a twenty-four–hour curfew for four days. Anyone found on the streets during this time would be shot on sight. He also announced the establishment of a Revolutionary Council to form a government until "normalcy" was restored.

The official reaction of the governments of the Commonwealth Caribbean was total shock. The reaction of the prime minister of Barbados, Mr. Adams, was given in a radio broadcast to the people of that island: "I was horrified at these brutal and vicious murders, the most vicious act to disfigure the West Indies since the days of slavery." While he indicated no specific course of action, he made it clear that he would have no dealings with a regime "stained by this record of murder."[25]

Other Caribbean politicians were equally outraged and expressed as much in their initial comments on hearing of Bishop's death. The worst fears of Caribbean leaders had been realized, and they reacted with urgency. Many pushed a suspension of all relations with the new government. A call for a boycott of the new government also came from the churches, trade unions, and other groups and individuals.

Prime Minister Adams of Barbados had taken the leading role in attempting to mount a rescue effort to free Bishop. But it was Prime Minister John Compton of St. Lucia who championed the idea of intervention by a multinational force. According to Mr. Adams, the day after Bishop and his colleagues were killed, "I was telephoned by Prime Minister Compton of St. Lucia who expressed himself in the strongest possible terms that the situation in Grenada could not remain as it was, and he proposed that there be a Caribbean initiative to intervene in Grenada on a multinational basis to restore law and order, and to lead the country to an early election."[26]

A number of Caribbean leaders had by this time concluded that intervention was the only reasonable way for them to deal with a situation that they perceived could affect them soon if it was prolonged or in the long run if a precedent of this kind was set. Their delay was a result of not having the men and material to undertake the job immediately. That their interests and those of the Reagan administration coincided, but for totally different reasons for each, is just plain politics.

Prime Minister Compton gave his analysis of events sometime later: although Caribbean governments disapproved of Bishop's authoritarian regime and his Cuban and Marxist connections, they were able to live with them. He had rid Grenada of Eric Gairy and had a popular following. "At meetings of the Caribbean governments in 1982 and 1983 he promised, under pressure, to hold elections and improve Grenada's human rights record. He seemed anxious to avoid regional sanctions, airline and currency restrictions, and exclusion from joint tourist advertising."[27]

Bishop's death changed that. Compton saw Bernard Coard as "a hard-line Marxist in the Stalinist mode" who could claim no popular following and would have shrugged off regional sanctions, turning to Cuba to "fill the void."[28] He saw Army Chief General Hudson as a front man for Coard. He saw the Grenada crisis culminating in Coard's engineering of General Austin's demise, "ostensibly in revenge for Mr. Bishop's,"[29] after which he would have "emerged with clean hands" as the leader of Grenada.[30] That, Mr. Compton felt, would have endangered every government in the Caribbean.

"We could not sit with Coard," Prime Minister Compton said. "We had to clean him out before he cleaned us out."[31] Compton's comments indicate the personal terms in which he saw the Bishop government and suggest that his tolerance for it was based to some extent on the ability of his colleagues, collectively and individually, to influence Mr. Bishop. He anticipated a loss of such influence under Bernard Coard. Another scenario mentioned by Caribbean scholars and diplomats was that, given Coard's dependence on the army, it could be expected that this well-politicized army would push Coard and the leaders with whom he was allied out and themselves seize power a few months later. This "revolt of the Majors," as they saw it, was a further reason why some politicians seemed to have concluded quite early that a military solution then was the only reasonable course of action to take.

After speaking to Prime Minister Adams of Barbados, Compton requested that the chairman of Caricom, Mr. Chambers, the prime minister of Trinidad and Tobago, call a meeting in Barbados to discuss the matter. Chambers summoned the meeting for Port of Spain, Trinidad, instead. It was the intention of Adams and Compton to hold an Organization of Eastern Caribbean States (OECS) meeting on Friday, October 21, and then, after deciding on a plan of action, to present a unified front at the larger Caricom meeting on October 22. The reason for pursuing such a strategy was clear. The smaller islands all were closer to Grenada and felt directly threatened by events there. Most had no standing armies and no militia of any consequence. Therefore their appeal to the larger Caricom members with standing armies had to be united if they were to convince them that action was needed, and quickly.

From Prime Minister Adams's later explanation, it is clear why he tried to insist that both the OECS and Caricom meetings be held in Barbados. "I first saw the High Commissioner for Trinidad and Tobago and explained to him, in confidence for transmission to his Prime Minister, that I would be unable to attend the meeting of the Caribbean heads of government the next day [October 22] in Trinidad since a military intervention in Grenada was being contemplated by the OECS with Barbados and other countries. I told him that my presence would be absolutely necessary in Barbados to conduct negotiations with countries taking part, and also to take such decisions on the military details as fell to the Chairman of the Defense Board."[32] Mr. Adams and the OECS countries were clearly already making informal plans for an invasion of Grenada before either meeting was formally convened. Later that day Mr. Adams also saw the British High Commissioner and the U.S. ambassador to inform them "what was contemplated," notifying them at the same time that "an invitation was likely to be extended" for them to participate. Later that afternoon the Canadian High Commissioner was also informed of the likely course of action "in deference to the outstandingly close relations of Canada and Barbados and the very high regard I have for Prime Minister Trudeau." That evening the OECS meeting was finally held.[33] First a formal meeting of the ministers of defense was held; then a meeting of the governing authority was called. It was "unanimously agreed to invoke Article 8 of the Treaty of Association and to seek the assistance of friendly countries to stabilize the situation and to establish a peacekeeping force."[34]

Because the Commonwealth Caribbean states feel a strong difference in culture, politics, institutions, and language from Latin states, their members feel a greater cohesion working within their own subregional grouping rather than within the Organization of American States. "It is important to note that neither Grenada nor any Eastern Caribbean country, including Barbados, is signatory of the 1947 Rio Treaty, and that the OAS is therefore ruled out as a peacekeeping body in our immediate area."[35]

Later that evening the chairman of the OECS countries, Prime Minister Eugenia Charles of Dominica, and Mr. Adams met Prime Minister Edward Seaga of Jamaica, who was in Barbados en route to the Trinidad meeting. They invited him to participate, and he accepted, but asked that a formal request be made in writing. Together the three "formally invited the participation of the USA through its ambassador."[36] According to Mr. Adams, it was purely coincidental that the United States task force bound for the Mediterranean was diverted to the Caribbean that very evening. But it goes to show how the two groups, the U.S. government and those of the Caribbean, were working toward the same action in a similar fashion.

It subsequently became known that the draft letter of invitation was actually prepared in Washington, D.C., and relayed to Barbados, where it was signed and then presented back to the U.S. government. One can only speculate that it was the desire of the U.S. administration to have a precise legal document in its hand that prompted it to compose its own draft. To others who dislike the notion of intervention, whether by invitation or not, such a maneuver had the smell of conspiracy about it. To still others, it showed that the United States was so distrusting of its partners that it could not rely on them to draft a simple letter. In the Commonwealth Caribbean, where its students have over the years won most of the highest honors every major British university has offered and from whence the British government chose several of its judges for its colonies in Africa, this did not go unnoticed.

The heads of government and the delegates arriving in Trinidad on October 22 had already made up their minds on a course of action and were attending this meeting of the larger regional grouping to involve their larger neighbors. Some of these states had already taken a position against Grenada and its new government. The prime minister of Trinidad and Tobago, after convening a cabinet meeting expressly to discuss the Grenada situation, called a press conference to convey his "shock and dismay" at the news from Grenada. He also announced that the government of Trinidad and Tobago had taken the following decisions with immediate effect until further notice:

1. Trinidad and Tobago would not participate in any CARICOM meeting whatsoever in which Grenada would be present;

2. No Grenada citizens or nationals would be allowed entry into Trinidad and Tobago without a visa;

3. No exports from Grenada into Trinidad and Tobago would be afforded CARICOM treatment and that no vessels registered in Grenada would be allowed the facilities of the Caricom Jetty in Trinidad and Tobago.[37]

He also said that the government would "take such steps as were necessary to ensure the safety of Trinidad and Tobago nationals in Grenada."

The OECS countries had decided against expelling Grenada from the organization, but they agreed to cease all cooperation with Grenada's new military rulers. Other sanctions were left to be taken up by the larger grouping of states.

The meeting opened as scheduled on October 22, 1983.[38] It was tacitly agreed before the meeting that the discussions would encompass everything except the military option, but this was a shortsighted exclusion since all the prime ministers and delegates either knew or had heard that intervention was being planned. This understanding was sought because in earlier consultations OECS leaders had ascertained that some of the heads of the larger states were not in agreement with the proposed actions of the smaller ones. However, the larger states realized that some sort of minimum action was necessary to register their own concern for the crisis in Grenada, if not agreement with the way the smaller islands were proposing to deal with it. Prime Minister Milton Cato of St. Vincent and the Grenadines told the conference that he had sent out feelers for possible talks with Commander Hudson Austin, the head of the new Grenada military council. But his colleagues would hear of no such overture, and that idea was promptly quashed.[39] Prime Minister George Chambers of Trinidad and Tobago explained his government's position, saying that he would have to seek parliamentary approval for action, but that he was against the use of force to resolve the crisis. Guyana was the only country that opposed every form of action, including the use of force. President Forbes Burnham was only prepared to commit troops to a peacekeeping force, and that only in a situation where the country's integrity was being protected, "but never to influence the political direction of a people." Little had really been expected from President Burnham. His opinion within the group in recent years had not carried the weight it formerly had. His handling of his country's economy, and even more his handling of opposition groups, had been a source of growing concern and embarrassment throughout the region.

Jamaica circulated a paper proposing major revision of the Caricom agreement. The OECS countries also circulated a paper proposing sanctions to be imposed against Grenada. Finally, it was agreed by most members present to support sanctions against Grenada. These included:

1. No official contact with the existing regime.

2. The regime would not be permitted to participate in the deliberations and business of the Organization.

3. Representatives of the regime would not be permitted to participate in or chair caucuses of groupings pertaining to meetings of International Agencies, and would not be permitted to speak on behalf of the OECS in international agencies.

4. The regime would not be allowed to benefit from the trade, economic and functional cooperation arrangements of the organizations.

5. No new issues of currency will be made to the regime under the East Caribbean Central Bank (ECCB) arrangements.

6. The OECS governments would cease all sea and air communication links with Grenada.[40]

As the conference dragged on into the early hours of the morning, it became clear that the prime ministers of the Bahamas, Belize, and Trinidad and Tobago and the president of Guyana were not in favor of military intervention. Nonetheless, within hours of the close of the conference, troops were being assembled in Barbados for an invasion of Grenada.

Clearly the smaller nations close to the orbit of Grenada felt more directly threatened than their larger associates. Their small size and the fragile nature of their societies compelled them to act rather than merely discuss their security and future. While intervention must have been abhorrent to contemplate, they had no alternative but to move to preserve their own security and well-being. That Prime Minister Adams of Barbados was willing to stake his personal reputation and that of his government and his people on the action of the OECS is an indication of his personal courage and his importance within the subregion. He undoubtedly knew from the beginning that the decision would be unpopular with some of his colleagues. Past events in the area and his appreciation for the fears and concerns of the ministates and for how much they depended on leaders like himself in such situations meant that he had to assume the leadership for planning the Caribbean invasion.

NOTES

1. The Bajan and South Caribbean (Bridgetown, Barbados), July 1982, pp. 4–6. For a different view of the meaning of the disturbances, see Albert Xavier, "Plotting That Had the Eastern Caribbean on Edge," *Wall Street Journal*, November 1, 1983, p. 30.

2. George F. Kennan, *The Nuclear Delusion: Soviet-American Relations in the Atomic Age* (New York: Pantheon Books), 1983, p. 192.

3. For a detailed explanation of the capricious way this act is applied, see Anthony Lewis, "Requiem for a Victim," *New York Times*, December 1, 1983 (the case of Professor Angel Rama of Uruguay).

4. Speech by Prime Minister J. G. M. Adams to the People of Barbados, *Nation* (Barbados), October 27, 1983, p. 16.

5. Ibid.

6. Ibid.

7. Ibid.

8. Interview with Donald McPhail, First Secretary, Grenada Embassy, Havana, reported by Joe Thomas, *New York Times*, October 30, 1983, p. 30. For an authoritative view and interpretation of events preceding and leading to the crisis, see Mohammed Oliver, "Grenada: Interview with George Louison," *Intercontinental Press* 22, no. 7 (April 16, 1984): p. 212.

9. Central Committee member George Louison gives the event as occurring on the last day of the meeting on September 16, 1984; Oliver, "Grenada: Interview with George Louison," p. 212.

10. Ibid.

11. Interview with Donald McPhail, First Secretary, Grenada Embassy, Havana, reported by Joe Thomas, *New York Times*, October 30, 1983, p. 20.

12. Ibid.

13. Ibid.

14. Arthur Schlesinger, Jr., "Foreign Policy and the American Character," *Foreign Affairs*, Fall 1983, p. 13.

15. *Trinidad Guardian*, Saturday, October 15, 1983.

16. Ibid.

17. *Trinidad Guardian*, Sunday, October 16, 1983.

18. Ibid.

19. See the transcript of the speech in *Trinidad Guardian*, October 19, 1983, pp. 22–24.

20. Ibid.

21. *Trinidad Guardian*, October 19, 1983.

22. Ibid.

23. *Barbados Advocate*, October 20, 1983. For a full text of the army's version of what happened, see *Nation* (Barbados), Special Grenada Evening Edition, October 20, 1983, p. 14. The top NJM members killed were Maurice Bishop, former prime minister; Unison Whiteman, former minister of foreign affairs; Jacqueline Creft, former minister of education; Norris Bain, former minister of housing; Vincent Noel, president of the Bank and General Workers Union; and Fitzroy Bain, president of the Agricultural and General Workers Union.

24. *New York Times*, January 6, 1984, p. A5.

25. *Barbados Advocate*, October 20, 1983.

26. *Nation* (Barbados), October 27, 1983, p. 16.

27. As reported by Tom Wicker, *New York Times*, November 18, 1983, p. A35.

28. Ibid.

29. Ibid.

30. Ibid.

31. Ibid.

32. *Nation* (Barbados), October 27, 1983.

33. The leaders present were: Antigua and Barbuda, Mr. Lester Bird, Deputy Prime Minister; Dominica, Mrs. Eugenia Charles, Prime Minister, Chrm.; St. Kitts-Nevis, Dr. Kennedy Simmonds, Prime Minister; St. Lucia, Mr. John Compton, Prime Minister; St. Vincent and the Grenadines, Mr. Milton Cato, Prime Minister; Montserrat, John Osborne, Chief Minister; Grenada, absent for obvious reasons. Barbados (Prime Minister Adams) was requested to attend the meeting and invited to participate.

34. *Nation* (Barbados), October 27, 1983.

35. Ibid.

36. The formal request was later made on October 23, 1983, to Jamaica, Barbados, and the United States.

37. Statement by the Honorable George Chambers, the Prime Minister, to the House of Representatives of the Parliament of Trinidad and Tobago, October 26, 1983, on the Grenada Crisis.

38. The Commonwealth Caribbean countries represented were: Bahamas, Barbados, Belize, Guyana, Jamaica, Trinidad and Tobago, Antigua, Dominica, St. Kitts-Nevis, St. Lucia, St. Vincent and the Grenadines, Montserrat, Grenada (absent).

39. Vincent Tulloch, *Daily Gleaner* (Kingston, Jamaica), October 26, 1983; see also *Sunday Guardian*, Trinidad, October 23, 1983.

40. Statement by the Honorable George Chambers, the Prime Minister, to the House of Representatives of the Parliament of Trinidad and Tobago, October 26, 1983, on the Grenada Crisis.

4

The Invasion: "Operation Urgent Fury"

Many observers expected the U.S. military to go into action somewhere soon, give the posture of the Reagan administration. Reagan had been elected promising to restore U.S. credibility, which implied the use of military power. Increased credibility was also the reason given for massive increases in the U.S. military budget for the preceding two years. Although the military seemed to dislike the idea of using military power to gain political ends, the civilian policymakers seemed to be eager for such an event.[1] Sending the fleet into disputed waters off Libya, into the Indian Ocean, and off Central America seemed to some to be a deliberate effort by the political and technocratic arm of the United States to draw some targeted nation into a skirmish to make a political point. This show of military strength by the Reagan administration prompted one eminent columnist to observe: "In a way, the great power game being played around the globe is made to order for an actor." But he warned:

The object is to do nothing for real. . . . Twice in the past four decades we miscalculated, and we had war in Korea and Vietnam. The worry now is whether Ronald Reagan can perceive the fine line between drama and reality.

Displaying military power, with all its bands and thunder, can become dangerously addictive. And dispatching battle units can begin to look like the cleanest, easiest exercise of power that a President can undertake.[2]

It is precisely this atmosphere that the Reagan administration had generated that caused many legislators and observers to challenge the administration's actions on Grenada. In the wake of the bombing and deaths of 256 marines in Beirut, suspicion was also thrown on the administration's motives for launching the invasion. Democratic Congressman Paul Simon of Illinois was among those who questioned the administration's sincerity. When asked about the invasion of Grenada, he said, "The military solution seems to be the automatic reflex with this administration."[3]

The news of the marines' deaths in Lebanon was a devastating blow to the Reagan administration's foreign policy and for the Middle East area in particular. Coming on the heels of a lengthy argument between the administration, the Congress, and the press about the role being played by the troops in Lebanon, the bombings were a grim reminder that esoteric arguments and political posturing are far removed from conditions abroad. While the status of the marines was debated—Were they peacekeepers or partisans?—to satisfy the War Powers Act, the different factions in Lebanon opposed to the presence of the marines had no illusions as to whose interests they were serving and who the intruders were. The marine commanders were given no clear method to keep the peace, and planning and fortifications by the commanders reflected the confusion of their role.

It was soon after this tragic foreign policy embarrassment that the Grenada decision was made. The atmosphere of uncertainty led to early challenges to administration explanations about events leading to the decision to intervene and the actual invasion itself. Whether or not the Reagan administration would have acted as it did in Grenada had the bombing in Beirut not occurred will be debated for some time to come; but the bombing unquestionably influenced the administration's decision.

Said House Speaker Tip O'Neill, "My honest opinion is that for the past two years the administration has been looking for an opportunity to get into Grenada . . . I just think it's wrong."[4] Senator Lawton Childs asked, "Are we looking for a war we can win?"[5]

Journalists on both sides of the Atlantic saw the invasion as a political act for Soviet consumption. One U.S. journalist offered this analysis of the invasion:

In a sense, the Reagan administration has been looking for a situation like Grenada from the day it took office. Senior foreign policy officials say that this is an administration that has felt a need—indeed, a compulsion—to demonstrate the use of American power, especially in the Western Hemisphere. . . . But the situation in Grenada presented the administration with the opportunity to take military action. Despite official statements that the prime motivation was to protect American citizens in Grenada, this operation, more than anything else, sends a strong message to both Nicaragua and Cuba that this is an administration that is ready and willing to use military force to achieve its objectives.[6]

A British journalist saw geopolitical and psychological reasoning behind the decision, which stemmed from American domestic political pressures:

As an option, the Grenada invasion was carefully, and almost publicly, prepared. The actual decision to go in—and without even the decorum of initial recourse to the United Nations—seems to have been taken in a hurry, following the massacre of more than 200 American marines in Beirut.

As the influential and sophisticated right-wing commentator William Safire puts it in the *New York Times*, "American military power is winning a victory in the Caribbean after suffering a humiliating defeat in Lebanon."

To respond to a bomb in Beirut by invading an island in the Caribbean makes excellent sense, in terms of the world-view of the Right, which is the view of many millions of Americans. Syria, seen as a proxy of the Soviet Union, is also seen as the country most likely to have been 'behind' the suicide bombings in Beirut. Cuba, seen as a proxy of the Soviet Union, is also seen as trying to take over Grenada. So, to punish the action of the less vulnerable proxy, by rebuffing and humiliating the more vulnerable one, is seen as an appropriate response and warning to the principal behind all of it: the Soviet Union.

The President is, of course, not just playing the Great Game on the international chessboard. He is also, and simultaneously, playing on the domestic board, a hardly less Great Game of being re-elected. . . . Reagan, of all men, cannot afford to look and sound like Carter, wringing his hands helplessly about the sad fate of Americans in some foreign country. After those bombings, Reagan had to do something, and quickly.[7]

The domestic pressure for the United States to reassert itself internationally had been a subject of domestic debate for some time. But it was candidate Reagan who implied that he would do so, and do so militarily. This some people found shocking in the second half of the twentieth century. It has also caused some scholars and journalists to argue that the sole purpose of U.S. foreign policy is to gain points domestically. Others see it as flowing naturally from the American system of government.

Some people think it shocking that an American President should be affected, in his international decisions, by domestic politics. Whether they are shocked or not, he will be so affected. One of the inconveniences of democracy, as a system of government, is that international decisions have to be made under the pressures of a public opinion which is only hazily informed about international affairs. This applies all round. It tends only to worry us in the case of the United States, because the United States is the biggest and the strongest, and the most democratic, of the democracies. And therefore the most dangerous.[8]

There was no absence of administration officials to defend and explain the decision, nor did the administration lack support within Congress. President Reagan personally briefed congressional leaders about the imminent invasion. Tip O'Neill was the first to break the ice: "God bless you, Mr. President," he said. "And good luck." He then gently patted Reagan's arm in a rare moment of rapport. Later he told reporters, "It's no time for the press of America or we in public life to criticize our country when our Marines and Rangers are committed."[9]

That such support should come from a leader of the opposition in the House, a man possessing dramatic ideological differences from the president, is symptomatic of the way leaders behave in a time of national crisis and decision making. It is also an indication of how the leaders see their role, how they come together to support the president after a decision to act abroad is made, and how they facilitate the working of the democratic system and process. It is an episode from which others in young democracies may learn. It was not until after Speaker O'Neill was certain that Grenada was taken and the marines safe that the partisan political debate started. O'Neill lashed out at the president's actions, saying, "We can't go the way of gunboat diplomacy. His policy is wrong. His policy is frightening."[10]

But the administration saw its role in slightly different terms. Secretary of State Shultz explained it this way: "If we want the role and influence of a great power, then we have to accept the responsibilities of a great power." True, but the advent of mass democracy in the world and a proliferation of new states, most of them non-European, make it the responsibility of a superpower to become aware of and responsive to other people. Failure to do so can be costly to any power in today's world, given the destructive capability of today's weapons. Short of totally obliterating a nation, a superpower unable to use its nuclear weapons as a threat to other nations has no particular advantage except credibility. Vietnam, Afghanistan, and Beirut are proof of that.

For the American body politic, the secretary of state observed, "This

may be a turning point in our history . . . we've let the world know that
we are going to protect our interest whatever the costs."[11] But the
administration was also concerned about its credibility in coming to a
decision on Grenada. "If we were asked by seven countries to restore
democracy in our own hemisphere and said no, who would ever believe
us or trust us again?" asked one senior White House aide.[12]

In the Caribbean itself, the interests of two groups came together—
those of the Caribbean states, especially the OECS countries, and the
United States. The decision to invade had already been made by the
OECS nations. What assurances they had of U.S. support at this time
is unknown. However, the United States, Canada, France, Britain, and
Venezuela were given every indication that such a decision might be
made when they were sounded out as possible senior partners in the
operation. U.S. policymakers were well aware of developments as they
proceeded to debate the developments in the Caribbean.

Within the Reagan administration, the president asked Vice President
Bush to convene the Special Situation Group to discuss the Grenada
developments. Strong concern was raised for the safety of the U.S.
citizens on the island; of primary concern were the 700 medical students
thought to be particularly vulnerable because of their high visibility on
campus facilities. With the hostage crisis in Iran still fresh in their
minds, the planners wanted to be sure that any action they took did not
jeopardize the safety of these U.S. citizens. It was agreed that the task
force en route to Lebanon be diverted to the Caribbean. This action the
secretary of state characterized as "a precautionary measure."

It seems clear from the reports of the events that followed and from
the position adopted by the administration once its decision had been
made that the safety of the students was not its most important concern
as it formulated its plans about how to react to the Grenada situation.
At this time the Reagan foreign policy advisers already knew that the
OECS countries were planning some type of military action to arrest
the problem. The United States had indicated that it would lend a
sympathetic ear to such a request, pending certain details. One was an
official invitation from the OECS countries to give the United States
firm legal ground on which to stand later. The other, it is surmised,
was a letter of invitation from someone in authority in Grenada itself—
the governor general.

The administration, realizing the implications of the act of invasion
given its earlier posture toward the Bishop government, needed to have

these legal trappings to bolster its defense against the barrage of criticism it knew it would face. True, there was some concern for the safety of the American students, but this concern was related to any other action which the United States might take. The administration had been given every assurance by those who claimed to be in authority that the students were in no danger. The administrators of the St. George's University Medical School in New York were in constant contact with the authorities and the students and staff on Grenada, and they felt these assurances to be sincere. The students themselves were afraid for their safety, as any group of foreigners would be when caught in a violent situation overseas, while the administrators were as concerned for their business and the possible effect renewed violence might have on it. Of course, the government of the United States has a right to be concerned over and to insure the safety of its citizens. But the United States could easily have airlifted the students to safety if this was its sole intention. The fact that the military commanders and soldiers did not know where the different sections of the campus were located even when they landed days later suggests that not much real effort was made to ascertain their exact locations. Rather, the United States wanted to be part of the invading force under the right circumstances. The opportunity presented itself in the form of an invitation from the OECS countries to participate with a Caribbean force in the invasion of Grenada to restore law and order. But each side needed the other for completely different reasons.

By accepting the invitation, the Reagan administration hoped to realize a number of political objectives it had been striving for. First, from the standpoint of principle it wanted to respond to a group of ministates that were genuinely concerned about the possible effect the breakdown of law and order could have in their democracies. By responding favorably, the administration hoped that the United States would again be perceived as a nation who was ready to stand by her democratic allies and friends. Second, it hoped to send a message to Central American states and others that the United States was once again willing to use its military might to enforce its interests and aid its friends. Third, it hoped to rid the U.S. domestic body politic of its reluctance to commit troops abroad, while at the same time showing President Reagan to be, as the American saying goes, "tough on communism." This would boost the image that the president's constituency had come to have of him for some time and fulfill an election pledge he had made to restore U.S. hegemony in the world. But it must be clear that despite U.S. pressure and intrigue in varying degrees through-out the life of the Bishop government, that was not what brought down the NJM, even though the tension and anxiety that it caused were real; the cause was internal squabbling for power.

For the Caribbean heads of the OECS countries and their partners, the invitation to the United States was clear. They did not intend to have the military takeover of politics and the overthrow of constitutional governments become part of the political process among the islands of the OECS. They had become more susceptible to this type of behavior, given their depressed economies and the way some politicians had used the system to thwart their opposition, and Grenada was a clear example. Lacking any internal or external impartial group or organization to stabilize such a situation, they were determined to act. Even if they themselves did not have the men and material to do the job, they were going to ally themselves with those who did.

On Friday, October 21, two U.S. consular officers and the deputy British High Commissioner visited Grenada to try to ascertain firsthand the political situation with the country and to make sure that the welfare of their citizens was being protected and assured. The military govern-ment of General Hudson Austin gave the diplomats every assurance that this was the case, but under the circumstances such assurances were accepted with reservations.

However, the conclusions drawn by the U.S. and British diplomats differed greatly. The House of Commons Foreign Affairs Committee reported it this way: "It is clear that the British High Commission's assessment of the danger of foreign nationals on Grenada was markedly different from that of the United States' consular officials . . . the United States officials regarding the Grenadian officials interviewed as obstruc-tionist and uncooperative."[13]

That evening President Reagan flew to Georgia for two days of va-cation at the Augusta National Golf Club. He was accompanied by Secretary of State George Shultz and Treasury Secretary Donald Regan. Secretary Shultz was awakened at 2:45 A.M. on Saturday with a cable from Barbados officially asking that the United States join the invasion of Grenada. Secretary Shutlz and NSC Adviser Robert McFarlane re-ported the request to Vice President Bush by telephone forty-five minutes later.[14] The vice president in turn roused other NSC members to discuss the request and reported to Secretary Shultz that the consensus was to speed up the planning for an invasion. At 5:15 A.M. President Reagan met with Secretary Shultz and NSC Adviser McFarlane to hear the request. He in turn wanted to get the views of Vice President Bush and Defense Secretary Caspar Weinberger and telephoned them personally.

In Washington Vice President Bush had initiated a meeting to begin at 9 A.M. He had assembled the top NSC officials, including Secretary of Defense Weinberger, General John Vessey, and key White House aides. The meeting lasted two hours, with the president joining in by speaker-phone from Georgia for the last five minutes. One participant summed up the discussion by saying, "Everyone was gung-ho." When one par-ticipant warned the president that there would be "a lot of harsh political reaction" to a U.S. invasion of such a tiny nation, the president replied "I know that. I accept that." But Defense Secretary Weinberger and Gen-eral Vessey wanted to learn more about the weapons the Grenadian military had, their willingness to fight, and the willingness of the Cubans.

In Georgia the president and the secretary of state deliberately stuck to their planned schedule so as to avoid alerting others to the planning going on in Washington. That afternoon a drunk gunman who wanted to see the president crashed his pickup truck through a golf course gate and took a number of people hostage in the pro shop. The president himself tried to speak to the man, but his attempts were fruitless.

His holiday weekend was again interrupted at 2:27 Sunday morning, this time with the tragic news of the bombings of the French and U.S. military headquarters in Beirut. The high number of casualties the United States suffered in Beirut, it is said, jolted him. As a result he departed for Washington early that morning for a round of NSC meetings. Al-though much of the talk at this time centered on Beirut, the bombing provided a good cover for planning of the Grenada operation. It also seems to have galvanized the politicians and policymakers to take a firm stand on Grenada; there was some fear that failure to act might be interpreted as a loss of will, especially by the island governments who had already been given tacit understanding that the United States would participate.

The next day, Monday, the U.S. embassy in Barbados received a note from the new Revolutionary Military Council of Grenada assuring the U.S. government that its citizens on the island were in no danger and would be permitted to leave if they wished. The U.S. State De-partment ignored the note, although by this time the Revolutionary Military Council of Grenada had been informed by a sympathetic head of state from the Caribbean area that a U.S.-Caribbean invasion was imminent. A few technocrats who had served in the Carter administration and who did not share the view of Reagan policymakers were doing their best to make the Revolutionary Council of General Hudson more acceptable to Washington and the Caribbean governments so as to forestall any invasion plans. At a final military planning meeting on that Monday, President Reagan gave his initial approval to proceed with arrangements for an invasion. With plans about to go into operation, the president called a meeting to brief key congressional leaders. This done, he spoke to Prime Minister Margaret Thatcher of Britain, informing her that the invasion was imminent and explaining his reasons. To his dismay she raised strong objections to the entire operation and suggested that economic sanctions might be more appropriate. Despite the protestations of this staunch ideological friend and ally, the president remained constant in his resolve. The next morning, October 25, 1983, operation "Urgent Fury" began. The objectives of the invasion were to protect and evacuate approximately 1,000 U.S. citizens, neutralize the Grenadian and Cuban forces, and stabilize the internal situation so that democratic government could be restored.

The actual battle plans were quite simple. The marines were to take the northern part of the island, including the operational Pearls airport. The rangers were assigned to capture the southern part of the island, including the medical school campus at True Blue and the new airport at Point Salines still under construction. The elite Navy Seals team was to slip into the environs of the capital and insure the safety of Governor General Sir Paul Scoon, capture the radio station, and free the political prisoners from the Richmond Hill prison.[15] Once these operations were completed, two battalions of army paratroopers were to be flown in for mopping-up operations and to secure all points for the 350-man Caribbean peacekeeping force.[16]

Preparatory ground operations for the actual invasion began late Sunday night and early Monday. At that time two small teams of Seals were sent to scout the island to identify suitable landing spots at both extremes of the island where the two airports were located. The group that scouted the Pearls airport area reported that there was no good spot for the marines' landing craft to come in. They recommended that Pearls be taken by helicopter assault. The other team sent to scout the Point Salines area never returned. One of the rafts was found swamped the next day.[17]

The first group to go ashore in the early hours of the morning of

October 25, the first day of the invasion, was the Navy Seals. They slipped ashore and made their way toward Government House, the residence of the governor general. His residence was under tight security, even though both the Bishop government and the Revolutionary Council had little use for him. Nevertheless, he was an important symbol, and his residence was always kept well guarded. At first the Seals were driven back by gunfire from the guards, but they counterattacked and quickly took charge of the residence.[18] Unfortunately, the key element of surprise hoped for was quickly lost on all fronts once the landings were made. According to the intelligence reports, a Cuban army colonel had arrived on the island a day earlier to prepare its defenses. "He did a damned good job," Admiral Joseph Metcalf admitted later. Once inside the governor general's residence, the Seals could not make the hasty retreat they had planned on. The Grenadian forces mounted their own counterattack on the governor general's house, advancing in three Soviet-built armored personnel carriers. At that point a U.S. Air Force Spectre, a C–130 transport fitted out with heavy rapid fire, was brought in. It took out the three armored personnel carriers, but the Seals were left trapped inside the house.[19] A stalemate then ensued, with no side making a move to test the other. "Gunfire around the house and the jail continued, frustrating further efforts to rescue Sir Paul Scoon and his protectors by air."[20]

"I was mad as hell about that," said Admiral Metcalf. At 11:45 the admiral called for an air strike on Fort Frederick, the suspected Grenadian command post. The strike destroyed Fort Frederick and accidentally blew up the mental hospital located next to the fort. The hospital was not shown on Admiral Metcalf's maps. Indeed, a lack of detailed maps of Grenada was a problem for the invading force. It was only when units of the invading force returned with maps they had captured from Grenadians that the planners had more detailed guidance in this area.

At this point, "Admiral Metcalf's deputy commander, Army Major General H. Norman Schwarzkopf, suggested that the best and probably the safest way to relieve the governor's house and the jail would be to reload part of the Marine unit on its transports and bring it around to the south part of the island, to a sandy beach north of St. George's."[21] This maneuver would take the better part of the following night to complete. The admiral agreed to the delay since the marines carried tanks, heavy guns, and trucks as opposed to the rangers and paratroopers, who were more lightly armed. He also knew that the governor general had twenty-two able men to protect him and could hold off an attack in case the house was attacked during the night. The tanks and other marine armor arrived and hit the beaches to take up positions at 7 P.M. that evening. The infantrymen themselves arrived much later, at 3 A.M. the next morning. At dawn, after a few rounds were fired to engage the enemy, it was discovered that the enemy had abandoned their emplacement. A marine convoy rescued Scoon and the commandos trapped with him, then discovered that the jail had also been abandoned.[22]

The rangers who were supposed to attack from the south to take the Point Salines airport flew from Savannah, Georgia, in C–130s and arrived at their drop zone at 5:30 A.M., a half hour behind schedule, having had problems with their navigational equipment.[23] At Point Salines the transport planes, with 500 rangers aboard, ran into a battery of antiaircraft and machine-gun fire. The lead plane was able to unload its paratroopers, but the next two planes had to circle back under cover from AC–130 gunships. In the heat of the exchange the planes came in too low, so the rangers had to jump from 500 feet, something not done by U.S. forces since World War II. As some of the rangers floated through the air, they were met by machine-gun fire.[24] The rangers, who thought that their operation would be a pushover, were quickly jolted into reality.[25]

One ranger recalled that once he had landed on the ground, "there was more fire to contend with, steady and well aimed, from positions that were cleverly placed in the surrounding hills. Whoever was up there, Grenadian or Cuban or both, knew how to fight."[26] Because of the heavy ground fire the Rangers called for an air strike. Meanwhile, some rangers began to clear the runway, which was barricaded by wire and construction vehicles left on the tarmac to prevent unauthorized landings. However, before planes could actually begin landing, the perimeter of security had to be expanded. The group pushed toward the Cuban construction workers' camp just beyond the airport itself, while another group made its way east toward the American medical students at True Blue. On their way the two groups encountered more resistance: one ranger was killed while manning a machine gun on the end of the runway, four others while setting up a roadblock to forestall reinforcements.

The rangers had secured a safe perimeter around the Point Salines airport by 7:15 A.M. and had secured the Cuban camp by midafternoon. They reached the medical school campus at 9 A.M. and found 130 students, safe but frightened. Once at True Blue the Rangers learned that the school had an even larger campus with 224 students at Grand Anse, halfway to St. George's, of which they had not been aware. Since the telephone system throughout the island was still functioning, they called the campus. The students warned that the rangers would probably have to fight their way in, as there were a number of strong points around the campus. Meanwhile, with the Point Salines airport open, troop reinforcements began pouring in by midday, including 1,600 paratroopers from the Eighty-second Airborne division. When a wounded Cuban officer said that there were about 1,100 well-trained Cubans on the island, a number far greater than the United States had anticipated, the planners decided to bring an additional 3,400 paratroopers.[27]

The Eighty-second Airborne took over the push toward the second campus at Grande Anse. Here the resistance was formidable. One paratrooper was killed in a firefight. Another died while inspecting a booby-trapped gun, and over a dozen were wounded. At 4 P.M. the rangers were loaded into marine helicopters in an attempt to engage the enemy coming through Grande Anse Bay from the undefended north. The choppers were set down in the middle of the campus, and the enemy was quickly outflanked. One helicopter was knocked out in this action, but its occupants were unhurt. In less than half an hour the operation was completed.

One objective still left was the barracks at Calivigny, on the east coast a few miles south of St. George's. It was not until the third day of the operation that the barracks was taken after heavy bombardment. By midday of October 27 the military situation was well in hand. The most that could be said of the operation was that it was a victory. It was a victory by troops who were well supplied and eager to prove their mettle. But it was a victory over Grenadian troops who found themselves in the middle of the most serious political and moral crisis they had ever had to come to terms with, badly trained and poorly equipped. The Cubans, it has been verified, were construction workers who were military reserves.

The invasion was not the swift surgical strike that policymakers in Washington like to talk about. It was neither swift nor surgical, given the disarray of the opposition they faced. The most that could be said was that the U.S. troops worked hard, persisted, and won what was surely an inevitable victory under the circumstances.

It serves no useful purpose to recount the litany of mishaps that took place during the invasion, but a few should be mentioned to complete the record. The failure of the U.S. military to know that the students they were trying to rescue had a main campus at Grand Anse seems typical of the misplaced emphasis and perception that plagued relations between the two countries from the outset. While President Reagan made decisions from aerial photographs from satellite surveillance, the military had no maps and did not know where the campus was located. The military was also plagued by more serious problems. The collision of aircraft, the bombing of their own positions, and other oversights in coordination pale by comparison with the episode in which the soldiers in the heat of battle fired the light, antitank weapons (LAWs) at the Russian-made armored personnel carriers and they failed to go off. Perplexed, the soldiers and officers wondered if the Russians were using some new metal or coat in their construction. The answer was much more elementary and closer to home: the LAWs being used were poorly constructed. While the soldiers were engaged in battle on October 25, the first day of operation Urgent Fury, the administration in Washington was engaged in a battle of another kind—explanation and defense.

NOTES

1. "Weighing the Proper Role," *Time*, November 7, 1983, p. 44.

2. Hugh Sidey, "How to Do Nothing Well," *Time*, August 22, 1983, p. 12.

3. "Weighing the Proper Role," p. 42.

4. *The Sunday Times* (London), October 30, 1983.

5. *Newsday*, New York edition, October 26, 1983, p. 3.

6. Jim Klurfeld, "Made to Order Action," *Newsday*, New York edition, October 26, 1983, p. 6.

7. Conor Cruise O'Brien, "Why the President Had No Choice," *Observer* (London), October 30, 1983, p. 8.

8. Ibid.

9. "D-Day in Grenada," *Time*, November 7, 1983, p. 28.

10. "Weighing the Proper Role" *Time*, November 7, 1983, p. 50.

11. "Weighing the Proper Role," p. 42.

12. "Americans at War," *Newsweek*, November 7, 1983, p. 55.

13. House of Commons, Foreign Affairs Committee, Second Report from Grenada, Session 1983–84, March 1984, p. xiv.

14. In this section I have relied heavily on *Time*, November 7, 1983.

15. The Navy Seals, as early Pentagon battle reports referred to them, were the Pentagon's new, elite, multiservice, antiterrorist force, the successor of the Delta Force used in the ill-fated Iran hostage rescue attempt. After the mission to Iran, the Pentagon expanded its joint commands force. It was given more money, more training, and more specialized soldiers from all three armed services, including the Navy Seals. So secret is this force that it is said that its very name is classified. John Fialka, "Battle for Grenada Commands Missions Didn't Go As Planned", *Wall Street Journal*, November 15, 1983, p. 1.

16. B. Drummond Ayres, Jr., "Grenada Invasion: A Series of Surprises," *New York Times*, November 14, 1983, p. A6.

17. Ibid.

18. *Time*, November 7, 1983, p. 25.

19. John J. Fialka, "Battle for Grenada Commands Missions," p. 21.

20. Ibid.

21. Ibid.

22. Ibid.

23. Ayres, "Grenada Invasion: A Series of Surprises," p. A6.

24. *Newsweek*, November 7, 1983, p. 66.

25. Ayres, "Grenada Invasion: A Series of Surprises," p. A6.

26. Ibid.

27. Ibid.

5

International Reaction and Administration Defense

First word of preparations for something in the area was picked up from the activities at the Barbados airport on October 24. On that day about fifty U.S. Marines arrived in Barbados in a naval transport plane, then flew off in three helicopters. Officials in Barbados and in Washington would not say where the troops were heading. Defense Department officials in Washington stated that the 1,800 marines who had earlier been diverted to the Caribbean had left for Beirut.[1] They did not say, however, that the entire task force had left the area, implying that some sort of action might still be possible. Meanwhile, U.S. and British diplomats who had gone to Grenada that day to inquire about the welfare of their citizens returned to Barbados with three U.S. citizens, the wife of a student at the St. George's University School of Medicine and two Peace Corps volunteers who were vacationing on Grenada. Fears and concerns were very strong, as the American parents of the students, fearful that their children would be caught in a crossfire, sent a telegram to President Reagan urging him to act cautiously.[2] Having become aware of this heightened concern for the welfare of civilians, the new military government assured the university chancellor of the safety of the students. Meanwhile, the U.S. embassy in Barbados sought to give the impression that the marines were poised in a forward position so as to be ready for an evacuation of the American students should this become necessary. The following day the true destination of the marines became known.

At a 9:00 A.M. news conference in Washington, President Reagan announced that he had ordered a predawn invasion of Grenada, where a "brutal group of leftist thugs violently seized power,"[3] killing the prime minister, three cabinet ministers, two labor leaders, and other civilians, including children. "Let there be no misunderstanding. This collective action has been forced on us by events that have no precedent in the Eastern Caribbean and no place in civilized society. . . . American lives are at stake, so we have been following the situation as closely as possible."[4]

The president's statement raised several questions. Most obvious was his sudden concern for the welfare of members of a government he had often criticized and sought to subvert. Certainly if protecting the lives of U.S. citizens was his main objective, other options could have been used to secure their release, either negotiation or a simple military airlift. But it was the prime minister of Dominica, Mrs. Eugenia Charles, who was present at the conference with the president, who aided Mr. Reagan at the questioning. In putting the Caribbean case to the press, she characterized the military operation as a "rescue" mission to restore law and order and, eventually, democracy to the island. Thereafter President Reagan latched on to this characterization of the event. But the administration's reasons for and accounts of the crisis differed as reporters were briefed at the White House, at the State Department, and at the Pentagon. Secretary Shultz saw the Grenada situation since the overthrow and murder of Bishop and his colleagues as dangerous: "We see no responsible government in the country . . . we see arrests of leading figures. We see a shoot-on-sight curfew in effect. . . . All of these things are part of an atmosphere of violent uncertainty that certainly caused anxiety among U.S. citizens, and caused the President to be very concerned about their safety and welfare."[5] Other officials said that concern for American lives heightened when the airport was closed.[6] Later it became known that the students could have left it they had desired to do so by charter flights still using the Grenada airport. General Austin's military government had attempted to assure the U.S. government as to the safety of its citizens, but was simply ignored.

Once these facts became known, the administration's case seemed weaker. In an attempt to justify its actions, the administration provided more reasons for taking such strong action. On the second day of the invasion, October 26, a senior administration official asserted that the invasion had forestalled a major Cuban military buildup on the island. He reported that a high-level Cuban delegation, similar to those sent by Cuba to Angola before the military buildup there, had arrived in Grenada on Monday.[7] This attempt to heighten the intensity and level of the threat to the United States and the conflict itself was recognized by a reporter who wrote: "At the start of the invasion early Tuesday, Administration officials estimated that about 600 Cuban construction workers were on the island. Today some officials talked of up to two battalions of Cuban troops, some manning anti-aircraft installations and otherwise 'well-armed and ready to fight.'"[8] The reporter also noted that "the Administration seemed more inclined today, in the face of strong foreign and domestic criticism, to cite the Cuban involvement as an extra justification for the American invasions. Reasons cited earlier were Washington's concern for the safety of American citizens and the request for intervention from some Caribbean island states."[9]

But by then it had become known (and the White House confirmed) that two days before the invasion Grenada's Revolutionary Military Council had offered the United States an opportunity to evacuate American citizens. Reagan administration officials, however, it was explained, distrusted the offer. This admission came from White House officials only after Grenadian officials released a copy of a cable sent by the Revolutionary Military Council to the U.S. embassy in Barbados stating: "The lives, well being and property of every American and other foreign citizens residing in Grenada are fully protected."[10] The piecemeal fashion in which the facts came out seems typical of politics in Washington, where officials offer changing and seemingly contradictory answers to the same event. On October 26, 1983, the first students from St. George's University School of Medicine arrived back in the United States and were overjoyed to be home.[11] In Grenada "they had felt isolated and uncertain following a violent coup" and welcomed an opportunity to return home.

On the whole, the students had nothing but praise for the president and the administration for extracting them from a difficult situation in safety. But the students were perhaps reacting more to the military situation than to conditions on the island prior to the invasion. To the foreign editor of UPI, who spoke to U.S. residents of the island by telephone, they reported that they were not being harassed by Grenadian security forces.[12] The school's chancellor, Mr. Charles R. Modica, speaking from his office in New York, saw the invasion as "very unnecessary" to save American lives and criticized this reason for the invasion. He insisted at a news conference that the safety of the students was assured by the new military rulers of Grenada. He went on to say that if Americans or citizens of any country were hurt by the invasion, the president "should be held accountable."[13]

Congress was still debating the debacle of Beirut when the president announced that the invasion was under way. Later in the afternoon Reagan formally notified Congress of the invasion, "consistent with the War Powers Resolution," but stopping short of invoking the section of the law that would require withdrawal of the troops within sixty to ninety days unless Congress approved it. In this letter to President Pro Tempore of the Senate Strom Thurmond, Mr. Reagan said that it was "not possible at this time to predict the duration of the temporary presence" of the troops on Grenada. He stressed, however, that "our forces will remain only as long as their presence is required."[14]

Congressional reaction to the announcement was restrained. Some of this was due to a desire not to compromise the president's domestic political position in executing his foreign policy, but partly it was due to the shock that the president, not yet out of the woods of the Lebanon disaster, had the temerity to undertake another bold foreign policy move of a military nature. They were stunned. Said Tip O'Neill: "We weren't asked for advice. . . . We were informed what was taking place." "One day we've got the number of Marine deaths . . . the next day we find we are invading Grenada," said Senator Lawton Childs. "This is an administration that shot first and asked questions later," commented Representative Thomas Downey. New York Senator Patrick Moynihan demanded that the administration explain how its actions conformed with the nation's international treaties.[15] He called the invasion "an act of war," then remarked, "I don't know that you restore democracy at the point of a bayonet."[16]

"While it is unfortunate that hostilities have broken out, it is also most important that Americans be protected," said Arizona Senator Barry Goldwater. Texas Senator John Tower noted: "It's a Marxist military dictatorship that engaged in murder to reach its ends." Senator Strom Thurmond said: "The lives of 1,000 Americans were directly threatened by the ruling junta in Grenada." And Senator Charles Percy stated: "Our hope is to have our forces out very quickly . . . as quickly as we can restore a semblance of order." Senator Lowell Weicker, after blaming the administration for the way it had treated Bishop when he visited Washington to try to mend fences a few months earlier, said: "I feel strongly the events of today need not have happened." He then added, "My support is totally minimal."[17] Senator Steve Symms commented: "This could be Ronald Reagan's Falklands Islands victory, signaling a welcome change in foreign policy . . . it is the first time in 20 years that we have tried to enforce the long-neglected Monroe Doctrine."

On the whole, the Congress was sharply split following the announcement that the invasion was under way, with supporters of the president applauding the move or simply saying nothing, but glad that the president was attempting to reassert American authority in a hitherto unresponsive and recalcitrant world. But opponents countered by deriding the president's "cowboy mentality" and his kneejerk reaction to solving political problems by military means. The overriding mood in Congress was astonishment, especially since the Pentagon news conference had announced that the U.S. forces had run into "some stiff pockets of resistance."[18]

Most stunned of all by the invasion was the press. It was shocked not by the invasion announcement itself, for a few had anticipated this possibility, but by the total blackout of the press coverage of the military and political situation as it was evolving on the ground in Grenada. Members of the press were incensed. They fumed at not being allowed to cover the invasion firsthand. The Pentagon maintained that military commanders had decided to exclude reporters from the invasion force in an effort to maintain secrecy and because their presence would complicate the force's logistical problems. Although there were vehement protests from editors, the military stuck to its decision and said that journalists would not be allowed onto the island for "two or three days."[19] Despite these arguments, the press knew that its Vietnam reporting had left a bad taste in the mouth of the military and that this exclusion was a new tactic of control.

In the face of continued protests from reporters and editors, the administration stuck to its position. At a news conference on October 26, 1983, Defense Secretary Caspar Weinberger maintained that the military commanders had decided that they did not want reporters along and added that he "wouldn't ever dream of overriding a commander's decision."[20] Other Defense Department officials, however, admitted that Britain's tight control over press coverage of the Falklands war had made a significant impression on American military commanders, particularly General Vessey, who had indicated in the past that there was too much coverage of the military by the press.[21] The exclusion of journalists from the first few days of action on Grenada was formally protested by the American Society of Newspaper Editors, who said in part that it went "beyond the normal limits of military censorship."

If the reaction of the Congress, the press, and the world was mixed or one of repudiation, the administration was heartened by the overwhelming support of the American people. Over half of the U.S. public approved of the U.S. participation in the invasion of Grenada.[22] This support must surely have been welcome comfort. Some saw this as a tendency to rally around the president during times of crisis and nothing else. It was a reaction to the specific foreign policy action and did not translate into blanket approval for his foreign policy generally or his domestic policy.

Further afield the Reagan administration did not fare well. NATO allies of the United States were particularly severe in their criticism of the invasion. They had viewed the Reagan administration's approach to dealing with the Bishop government from afar and had disapproved in silence. Attempts by the Reagan administration to have EEC countries boycott an aid donor's conference to raise money for the building of the international airport were unsuccessful. Europeans were also aware of the administration's actions at the World Bank and the IMF to try to have those international organizations refuse loans to the Bishop government. Despite these pointed moves, the EEC countries provided some of the financing that Grenada badly needed.

It was against this background that most European governments viewed the steady decline of U.S.-Grenada relations in 1983. Invasion was seen as a logical extension of covert attempts to bring down the government of Grenada. European condemnation of the invasion itself was almost unanimous. French president François Mitterrand saw it as "a surprising action in relation to international law." West German chancellor Helmut Kohl issued an uncharacteristically blunt statement, saying in part: "If we had been consulted, we would have advised against it." Italian prime minister Bettino Craxi noted that U.S. intervention "has dangerous precedents and also establishes another dangerous precedent." Although European governments objected in principle to the invasion, they were even more concerned about the likely effects of the U.S. action on the still-simmering controversy to deploy U.S.-built Pershing II and cruise missiles on their territories within a few months. They were anxious not to be too harsh on the

United States for fear of arousing a more generalized disaffection, the consequences of which could be disastrous.

It was the British, however, in view of the past and present relationship with Grenada and their "special relationship" with the United States, who felt rebuffed in the whole affair. The ensuing argument is a prime example of how a minor crisis in a small country can threaten and even destroy an alliance and will be looked at in depth in chapter 7.

No group of nations was more incensed about the U.S.-led invasion than those in Latin America, and with good reason. They had been the object of U.S. intervention far too often in the past, intervention that had often stunted their political growth and maturity and left many angry and frustrated. Most U.S. interventions in Latin America were designed to preserve the power of the ruling oligarchy, not, as in the case of Grenada, to prevent elite conflict from degenerating into civil war. But Latin Americans were frustrated that after a prolonged period of neglect by Washington, U.S. involvement in the area should be military action in Grenada and a threatened action in Central America. The most active secretary of state, Henry Kissinger, admitted this neglect when he said: "Our minds have been east and west . . . For me, going to Mexico was a long distance, but going to Europe was nothing."[23]

Grenada, though belonging to the Western Hemisphere region geographically, is a member of a subregion with a distinct identity and peculiarities and one that never wanted to be measured by the same standards as other Latin American states. The Commonwealth Caribbean states are different from other Latin American states in the following respects:

1. The population speaks English.
2. There has never been a successful military coup.
3. Grenadians have always expressed a desire not to be considered Latin American culturally.
4. They share a number of experiences culturally and politically and support a number of economic and cultural institutions common to their group.
5. They hold elections regularly.
6. They share a common judicial system.
7. They share a common university system.

So while Latin American fears were real, Latin Americans were influenced by their own harsh experiences and by what they saw as a tendency of a new, more hawkish U.S. administration.

Upon the announcement of the invasion, Latin American nations used two forums to make their views known, the Organization of American States and the UN. Several Western and Latin American diplomats felt that the reasons given by President Reagan for his decision to send troops to Grenada could just as easily be applied to Nicaragua and its Sandinista government.[24] Other Latin American officials saw the invasion as a warning to the government of Nicaragua. In Nicaragua itself the foreign minister summoned the diplomatic corps to his office and read them his government's position. It said in part that the invasion was "a new demonstration of imperial arrogance" by the United States. It went on to say that "nothing justifies the intervention of North American troops nor the immoral arguments put forward to justify their invasion."[25] In an urgent session of the Security Council of the United Nations, requested by Nicaragua with the support of Guyana, both nonpermanent members of the council, one delegate observed: "There is a sense of alarm about the situation. . . . We don't know what we're in for, where all this will lead."[26]

At the UN Security Council meeting on October 25, the United States seemed to have gathered little sympathy for its case. One delegate from a nonaligned state summed up the consensus this way: "If you go by the general mood in the corridors, there is a feeling that what has happened is very disturbing and that the Americans are rather isolated. . . . Some countries may not want to speak out about it, but they are disturbed about what has happened and they are not very satisfied with the explanations given."

The United States had tried unsuccessfully to have the debate postponed until the Caribbean leaders could be present. When the debate opened, the Nicaraguan delegate gave a speech chronicling the history of American intervention in Latin America beginning in 1846. Mrs. Jeane Kirkpatrick labelled the charges as "examples of projection" and criticized the government of Nicaragua for its actions in Central America. "I think it is doubtless true that the Government of Nicaragua cannot imagine a government having great strength and not using it against hapless, helpless neighbors. . . . The Government of Nicaragua, having small strength, uses it in an uninhibited fashion against its neighbors and imagining that everyone and all countries would behave that way is obviously concerned about having more powerful neighbors."[27] She went on to reiterate the position of the Reagan administration.

Ambassador Kirkpatrick's rush to attack the government of Nicaragua did little to advance the position of the Reagan administration. It did show the U.S. preoccupation with Nicaragua's behavior in the region, which had challenged the U.S. strength and intentions and had forced the UN session in the first place. But if the Reagan administration had been inconsistent in explaining its motives—mixing its opposition to communism with an apparently legitimate request for help from a group of tiny democracies—it got some much-needed help from the chairman of the OECS, Prime Minister Eugenia Charles of Dominica. She announced that the British-appointed governor general of Grenada, Sir Paul Scoon, had asked the OECS "for aid" after the assassination of Bishop a week earlier. Mrs. Charles explained that that information could have been released only after Scoon's safety had been assured by the U.S.-led invasion force.[28] Although the governor general has only ceremonial duties and almost no power, as the figurehead of state his influence and advice is sought and respected.

Mention of this appeal for assistance was the first inkling the world got that the people of Grenada had in some way sanctioned the invasion. Mrs. Charles went on to tell the Security Council that the Caribbean countries had viewed events in Grenada leading up to the invasion as a threat to their security.[29] She took pains to stress the feelings of the governments and people of the area and the security threat that they felt developments in Grenada posed. She seemed to purposely avoid drawing any relationship with unsubstantiated Cuban and Communist intentions. Charles was supported by a sister Caricom and OECS member, Antigua. The delegate from Antigua and Barbuda, Mr. Lloydston Jacobs, said that after the murder of Bishop, the Grenada regime "had foisted on the backs of our black brothers and sisters a junta with Cuban and Russian advisers."[30] Mrs. Charles's revelation that the governor general of Grenada had appealed for help was taken at its face value, but strong evidence emerged subsequently to suggest that her story was not quite true. Much of the British press and the British parliamentary investigation questioned the existence of any such letter; they asserted that the real urgency in rescuing Sir Paul and rushing him onto the aircraft carrier was the need to have him belatedly sign the aforementioned letter.[31] Here again, the Reagan administration was to be caught up in a conflict between legality and principle, further contributing to a problem with credibility among both its allies and its detractors.

The support of the OECS countries for the U.S. position helped to moderate the tone of the debate on the second day of the Security Council session. But feelings about the invasion were still high. The debate continued. On the third day of the debate, the United States was due to reply to the charges made by many of the nations who spoke. Before speaking, the United States challenged the right of Ian Jacobs, the Grenadian delegate, to participate, citing a letter from Sir Paul Scoon requesting that no one be allowed to represent Grenada in the council's deliberations. But the president of the Security Council, Mr. Abdullah Salah of Jordan, ruled that Mr. Jacobs should take his seat pending a decision by the secretary general of the United Nations.[32]

In her response to the charges made by delegates that invasion violated international law, Mrs. Kirkpatrick said: "The prohibitions against the use of force in the United Nations Charter are contextual, not absolute. They provide justification for the use of force against force, in pursuit of other values also inscribed in the Charter, such values as freedom, democracy and peace. . . . The Charter does not require that people submit supinely to terror nor that their neighbors be indifferent to their terrorization."[33] She also cited the strong Cuban presence and military buildup on the island as "foreign intervention" that had occurred long before the United States landed. "The familiar pattern of militarization and Cubanization was already far advanced in Grenada," she said, referring to the arsenal of weapons found by the invading force and the large number of technical and military personnel on the island. But the Reagan administration's attempt to cast the invasion effort in anticommunist terms was not convincing and seemed more designed to satisfy the domestic constituency. When the resolution before the Security Council, "deeply deploring" the U.S.-led invasion and labelling it a "flagrant violation of international law," was voted on, the United States vetoed it.[34] Eleven countries voted for the resolution.

Britain, Togo, and Zaire all abstained from voting, while France, the Netherlands, and Pakistan—all allies of the United States—voted for the resolution.[35] The vote was an indication of how strongly most nations felt about the U.S.-Caribbean action and how the United States failed to persuade even its allies as to the rightness of its cause. Not even President Reagan's explanation on television on October 27 seemed to change the minds of the delegates. The vote was a victory for those countries who were the main movers to isolate and embarrass the United States in the world forum: Guyana, Nicaragua, and Zimbabwe. Of the sixty-three nations that addressed the council, only the Caribbean nations involved in the invasion supported the United States.

Reagan had gone on television on October 27 to bolster the administration's conflicting and unraveling defense of its actions in Grenada. In his speech he gave a brief history of the political developments of the area of Grenada, referring to Maurice Bishop as a "protégé of Fidel Castro." He explained the difficulty with Maurice Bishop:

He sought to help Cuba in building an airport, which he claimed was for tourist trade, but which looked suspiciously suitable for military aircraft, including Soviet-built long-range bombers. The six sovereign countries and one remaining colony are joined together in what they call the Organization of Eastern Caribbean States. The six became increasingly alarmed as Bishop built an army greater than all of theirs combined.

Obviously it was not purely for defense. In this last year or so, Prime Minister Bishop gave indications that he might like better relations with the United States. He even made a trip to our country and met with senior officials at the White House and the State Department. Whether he was serious or not we'll never know.[36]

In the light of the evidence to the contrary, it is amazing that Reagan could come to such conclusions. The United States had to know that the airport was being partly financed by the British and other European governments. While no one would doubt that Grenada might lend its airport facilities to countries the United States might not approve of, there was nothing about the airport to suggest that it was for military use and not for tourism as Grenada had asserted. That the neighbors of Grenada were troubled by the increasing military buildup was natural. However, they had enough clear evidence of U.S. measures against the Bishop government to realize that Grenada had perceived itself to be under constant pressure from the Reagan administration, and that the military buildup was in response to this. Bishop's contact with other radical elements in the Caribbean and subsequent statements by some leaders of these groups gave the tiny island governments cause for concern even as they fought in other forums to protect the rights of the Grenadian people. They seemed prepared to brook the natural emergence of domestic opposition, but were totally against comparing them-

selves to the Grenadian model or having any solidarity contact with that
government and party.

While the governments of the Caribbean saw the problem as one of
domestic politics, President Reagan saw it in anticommunist terms. He
summed up his speech to the American people in this way:

Grenada, we were told, was a friendly island paradise for tourism. Well, it
wasn't. It was a Soviet-Cuban colony being readied as a major military bastion
to export terror and undermine democracy.

We got there just in time.

He also attempted to portray the bombing of the marines in Lebanon
and the invasion of Grenada as parts of a grand design by the Communists: "The events in Lebanon and Grenada, though oceans apart,
are closely related." This was rather farfetched in view of the political
history of both countries. The speech itself did not succeed in making
coherent the administration's reasons for mounting the invasion. However, it did boost the morale of Americans and Caribbean allied leaders,
all of whom were perturbed by the length of time the operation seemed
to be taking and by reports of stiff resistance and possibly continued
guerrilla warfare. The Caribbean leaders were particularly anxious about
these reports, as they were very sensitive that a prolonged stay by U.S.
troops in the area could present serious problems for them politically.
So even though the Reagan administration would have preferred to wait
and make a grand announcement of a victory by its fighting men,
political pressures forced the president to make an earlier-than-planned
appearance to explain and affirm the U.S. position rather than claim a
victory. Despite the administration's attitude, questions still remained.
Having stated that the safety of Americans on Grenada was the first
reason for the U.S. participation in the invasion, Reagan asserted that
he had reports that "a large number" were "seeking to escape."[37]
Administration officials told the press that the Grenadian regime had
closed its airport, implying that there was no way for Americans to
leave and raising the possibility that they could be held hostage.[38] But
shortly after, it was learned that the airport was open and that Americans
had flown out on a normal commercial carrier the day before the invasion, encountering no problems at the airport. Later it also became
known that Grenada and Cuba both had sent urgent messages to the
United States saying that its citizens, in particular the large number of

medical students, were safe. But these assurances were not given any weight by the administration, apparently because the administration was intent on a military course and was determined not to delay the operation for cooperative enemies.

When the administration first gave its reasons for the invasion, there was no mention of a Soviet-Cuban/American rivalry. One political columnist challenged the link the president was trying to draw. "The statement was no doubt effective politically. It would be hard to find language better calculated to play on American fears than 'Soviet Cuban colony' or 'military bastion' or 'terror.' But where is the evidence for those assertions?"[39] The administration was able to offer little real evidence of Soviet-Cuban intentions to use the island as a base for subversion throughout the area. This fictionalizing was based more on a hungering of the United States to reassert itself in this hemisphere and around the world. Admiral Wesley L. McDonald, commander in chief of the U.S. Atlantic Fleet, expressed this attitude in a statement to members of Bishop's and other splinter groups on Grenada. "We have to identify the people who are hard-liners," he said. "I think the identification process is going to be one that is very difficult for us to continue to pursue, but one that we've got to do because we cannot afford the withdrawal of all of the forces and allow an insurgency government to reappear."[40]

There were some who did not think that the administration ought to be involved in the security affairs of the island and in determining what type of government emerged thereafter. What purpose could be served by foisting an unpopular government on people who had just gone through a crisis to deter exactly that?

No aspect of the administration's explanations of the invasion caused greater reaction than its explanations of the Cuban presence in Grenada. But as the invasion progressed, the Cubans' presence and retaliation against the invading American troops became a central part of the administration's reasons for its action. Maurice Bishop's friendship with Fidel Castro and the government of Cuba was the primary reason for U.S. hostility toward the Bishop government through the administrations of both Carter and Reagan.

The U.S. government had notified Cuba and the Soviet Union of the invasion "as the operation got under way." The United States also announced its "readiness to look to the safety of their people on the island."[41] The Soviets on the island, about 30 in number, were quickly identified and corralled. The almost 600 Cubans, however, were mainly concentrated near the new airport they were constructing. They put up stiff resistance to the invading force, and a Cuban was quoted by the Associated Press as saying on the first day of fighting on Grenada, "At nightfall the heroic resistance of our constructors and collaborators continued."[42] The fierce fighting of the Cuban construction workers surprised the invading force; they were obviously well trained, well directed, and prepared. That they would put up such strong resistance in the face of such overwhelming odds amazed some and confirmed the opinion of some of their detractors who insisted that they were indeed soldiers.

The question was raised by a reporter to Secretary of State Shultz about the possibility of Soviet or Cuban involvement in the coup that precipitated the invasion. To this he replied: "We don't have any direct information on that point. However, the OECS states feel that such is the case. But it is not the basis of this action on our part."[43] But by the second day of the invasion the Cuban presence on the island began to emerge as a central part of the administration's justification for its action. "Reagan Aide Says U.S. Invasion Forestalled Cuban Arms Buildup," cried one paper's headline. Another headline read: "Cuban Troops Called Surprise to U.S." On the first day of the invasion administration officials estimated that there were about 600 Cuban construction workers on the island. By the second day officials were talking of up to "two battalions of Cuban troops [1600 soldiers], some manning anti-aircraft installations and otherwise 'well-armed and ready to fight.' "[44] The notion that there might be "Cuban fighting units" was unsubstantiated and appeared obviously to bolster the administration's position in the face of heavy criticism.[45]

"I honestly believe we got there just in time," said one senior official. "The judgment was that the Cubans were about to bring troops into Grenada just as they had done in Angola in 1975. On the day before the U.S. decision to act, a high-level Cuban delegation arrived in Grenada. That is close to the scenario in Angola before there was a commitment of Cuban troops."[46] Having planted the seed of heavy Cuban military involvement in the fighting on an island about to be subjugated, administration officials cultivated a mindset for President Reagan's analysis and speech on October 27, 1983.

From Havana, however, the reaction was different. Fidel Castro had announced that his people would not surrender, and government radio proclaimed that the Cuban resisters planned "to fight to the last man and the last bullet." Castro condemned the U.S.-led invasion, calling it an "enormous political error" in which there was "no logic."[47] He said also that "there was no risk to Americans and special measures had been taken for their safety by the Grenadians." Castro claimed that it was "no secret" that the Cubans were helping to build an airport at Point Salines. He categorized the Cubans on the island as 550 construction workers, including doctors, professors, and agricultural technicians. He admitted that another 40 Cubans were military advisers, calling the number "very small." When asked about relations between his government and that of the new Grenadian regime, he said that they were "extremely cold and, to a certain degree, tense."[48] But Cuban casualties were high, and they did surrender after having been overwhelmed by the invading U.S. troops. Although the Cuban government tried to put a good face on it, their defeat and expulsion was a severe blow to Castro's policy in the Caribbean area.

By the third day of the invasion the major objectives were complete but for some Cuban and Grenadian troops who decided to fight a guerrilla war. Cuba, having no diplomatic relations with the United States, announced that it had accepted an offer from Colombia and Spain to mediate the return of Cubans taken prisoner in Grenada. Arrangements were also worked out for the return of the wounded and dead to their homeland. On the fourth day of the invasion the Reagan administration again increased its estimate of the number of Cubans on Grenada to 1,100 while admitting that confusion on the ground in Grenada made it impossible to provide a precise count.[49] This increase was made in the midst of growing debate as to why the intelligence agencies of the United States had failed to measure Cuban strength on the island more accurately before the invasion. Some military officers had complained privately that the gap in intelligence seriously handicapped planning for the invasion and left the troops unprepared for the intense resistance they faced from the heavily armed Cubans.[50] Admiral Wesley L. McDonald, commander in chief of American forces in the Atlantic region, was cautious at a Defense Department news conference. After noting that "resistance was much greater than expected due to the extensive Cuban military involvement on the island," he said: "I didn't have enough intelligence but I don't think there was a failure there."

None of the initial reasons given by President Reagan to justify the invasion turned out to be quite true. It was later proved that the Cubans were not heavily armed and that they fought well because of their training as members of the reserve, not because they were part of their country's army as was suggested. As it later turned out, Fidel Castro was the only person who was telling the truth all along, a point overlooked by the U.S. press, which chose to give credence instead to the administration's assertions. The well-publicized photos of the medical students returning to the United States in military aircraft and kissing the ground as they disembarked imbued the administration's position with strong emotional validity, even while the press was deliberately excluded from covering the fighting itself in Grenada. (Although the press made its displeasure known, this did not keep it from faithfully reporting the administration's version of the war.)

But for all the disagreement and rancor that the decision to invade Grenada brought upon the Reagan administration, it must have felt satisfied about one thing: the steady backing it received from the governments and people of the area itself. Throughout the Commonwealth Caribbean there was nothing but overwhelming support.

NOTES

1. Michael T. Kaufman, "50 Marines Land At Barbados Field," *New York Times*, October 25, 1983, p. 1.

2. Ibid.

3. Press conference by President Reagan, October 26, 1983.

4. Text of Reagan's announcement of the invasion, *New York Times*, October 26, 1983, p. A16.

5. Hedrick Smith, "Cubans Clash with Force—30 Soviet Advisers Are Reported Safe," *New York Times*, October 26, 1983, p. 1.

6. Ibid.

7. Hedrick Smith, "Reagan Aide Says U.S. Invasion Forestalled Cuban Arms Buildup," *New York Times*, October 27, 1983, p. A1.

8. Ibid.

9. Ibid.

10. Ibid.

11. Fay S. Joyce, "First Evacuees Arrive in U.S. from Grenada," *New York Times*, October 27, 1983, p. 1.

12. Jonathan Friendly, "Reporting the News in a Communique War," *New York Times*, October 26, 1983, p. A23.

13. "John T. McQuiston, School's Chancellor, Says Invasion Was Not Necessary to Save Lives," *New York Times*, October 26, 1983, p. A20.

14. Susan Page, "Reagan: No Choice But Decisive Action," *Newsday*, New York edition, October 26, 1983.

15. Judith Bender, "Congress Takes Hard Look at Battle Lines," *Newsday*, (New York), October 26, 1983.

16. Steven V. Roberts, "Capitol Hill Sharply Split Over the Wisdom of Invading Grenada," *New York Times*, October 26, 1983, p. A22.

17. Bender, "Congress Takes Hard Look at Battle Lines."

18. B. Drummond Ayres, Jr., "Defense Dept. Says the Marines and Rangers Quickly Achieve Initial Goals," *New York Times*, October 26, 1983, p. A22.

19. Friendly, "Reporting the News in a Communique War."

20. Phil Gailey, "Administration Puts Tough Restrictions on News of Grenada," *New York Times*, October 27, 1983, p. A1.

21. "Keeping the Press from the Action," *Time*, November 7, 1983, p. 65.

22. "How the Public Sees It," *Newsweek*, November 7, 1983, p. 65.

23. Hugh Sidey, "Needed: New Compass Settings," *Time*, May 9, 1983, p. 35.

24. Richard J. Meislin, "Regional Neighbours Predict Broad Effect from Action," *New York Times*, October 26, 1983, p. A19.

25. Ibid.

26. Richard Bernstein, "Latins in U.N. Council Assail the U.S. Invasion," *New York Times*, October 26, 1983, p. A18.

27. Richard Bernstein, "Grenada Debate Continues in UN," *New York Times*, October 27, 1983, p. A19

28. Ibid.

29. Ibid.

30. Ibid.

31. *New Statesman* (London), November 4, 1983, p. 8.

32. Bernstein, "Grenada Debate Continues in UN," p. A19.

33. Ibid.

34. Richard Bernstein, "U.S. Vetoes UN Resolution 'Deploring' Grenada Invasion," *New York Times*, October 29, 1983, p. A1.

35. Ibid.

36. Ronald Reagan, televised speech, October 27, 1983.

37. Anthony Lewis, "What Was He Hiding?" *New York Times*, October 31, 1983, p. A19.

38. Ibid.

39. Ibid.

40. Ibid.

41. "Transcript of Shultz's News Conference on Why U.S. Acted," *New York Times*, October 26, 1983, p. A18.

42. Smith, "Cubans Clash With Force—30 Soviet Advisers Are Reported Safe."

43. "Transcript of Shultz's News Conference on Why U.S. Acted," *New York Times*, October 26, 1983, p. A18.

44. Smith, "Reagan Aide Says U.S. Invasion Forestalled Cuban Arms Buildup."

45. "General Vessey, Excerpts from News Conference of Secretary of Defense," *New York Times*, October 27, 1983, p. A18.

46. Philip Taubman, "Cuban Troops Called Surprise to U.S.," *New York Times*, October 27, 1983, p. A20.

47. "Cubans Defending Outpost Died Heroes, Havana Says," (A.P.) *New York Times*, October 27, 1983, p. A20.

48. Ibid.

49. Philip Taubman, "U.S. Now Puts the Strength of Cubans on Isle at 1,100," *New York Times*, October 29, 1983, p. A6.

50. Ibid.

6

Caribbean Reaction

The government of Trinidad and Tobago favored some action against the new Grenada regime, but was absolutely opposed to the invasion coming before diplomacy had been tried. As a result, it did not contribute troops to the operation. But a survey conducted by the St. Augustine Research Associates for the *Trinidad Express* newspaper gives an insight into the feelings of the general public.

1. Do you think that military force should have been used to settle the Grenada problem, or should efforts have first been made to negotiate a solution with the Revolutionary Military Council?

   (a) Force was the only alternative—63 percent

   (b) Negotiate first with the RMC—28 percent

   (c) Don't know or no opinion—9 percent

2. Do you think the decision to invite the United States was justified or should the invading force have included Caricom states only?

   (a) U.S. invitation was justified—61 percent

   (b) Caricom states only—20 percent

   (c) Don't know or no opinion—19 percent

3. Do you think that Trinidad and Tobago should have joined the invasion?

   (a) Yes—56 percent

   (b) No—32 percent

   (c) Don't know or no opinion—12 percent[1]

The overwhelming response to the poll suggests the extent to which most people in Trinidad and indeed in the Commonwealth Caribbean knew of the Grenada situation and had some opinion of what should be done about it.

Support in Trinidad for the invasion also came from the opposition leader of the Organization for National Reconstruction, Mr. Karl Hudson-Phillips, a former attorney general. He gave his views at a political meeting. "A lot of noise is being made in certain (unnamed) quarters about the principles of international law and the question of non-intervention in the affairs of another state. . . . Nowhere is it stated that this (non-intervention) principle is an absolute principle not admitting to any exceptions whatsoever."[2] He then added as an exception what he called "humanitarian intervention." He interpreted this as follows: "When a state or country is guilty of cruelties against and persecution of its nationals in such a way as to deny their fundamental human rights and to shock the conscience of mankind, intervention in the interest of humanity is legally permissible." He pointed out that "there is a substantial body of opinion and of practice in support of the view that there are limits to the manner in which a sovereign country can treat even its own citizens."[3] He offered as an example East Africa: "There is no quarrel with Tanzania for its intervention in Uganda to assist in the removal of Idi Amin." But not everyone in Trinidad was unequivocal in their support of the invasion. Another former high-ranking official of the government, Dr. Patrick Solomon, gave the invasion only limited support, and even though he welcomed the end result, he wrote: "The predominant feeling in Trinidad and Tobago will be one of happiness that our brothers in Grenada have been released from the yoke placed upon them by the madmen and murderers who executed Maurice Bishop and most of his Cabinet, and I share that feeling of joy; but, from then on, I part company with the majority, for there is no way the invasion of Grenada by foreign troops (even if Caricom forces are involved) can be justified in law."[4] The Trinidad and Tobago Students Union and the West Indies Group of University Teachers both condemned the invasion, deplored the "violation of the sovereignty" of Grenada, and called for a withdrawal of all foreign forces from the island.[5]

But one well-known political columnist castigated them all, including the press, for their hypocrisy. He claimed that it was "obscene" the way in which the press and the country "suddenly saw virtue in a man [Bishop] whom many of them had castigated for four and a half years."

He expressed no surprise, said that he shed no tears over Bishop's death, and claimed that events as they concluded in Grenada were likely to end the way they did, given the political system Bishop himself had built and extolled. He saw it as an "inevitable method of settling political differences in the absence of established constitutional procedures" that Bishop himself had dismantled. He noted that he, as an independent-minded journalist, would not have been able to function in Grenada. He accused one faction of supporting a position where "they had been helping Bishop and the New Jewel Movement to remove a constitutionally secure tyrant from office, and then later to help bolster and insulate the leftist NJM regime from the attacks of advocates of Western-style democracy."[6] For this he blamed the Oilfield Workers Trade Union of Trinidad and Tobago, a union very close and sympathetic to Bishop and the NJM, and a number of other unions, including the academics and student organizations of the University of the West Indies at St. Augustine. The commentator also took to task the prestigious *Trinidad Guardian* newspaper. He accused it of appealing to the emotions of the people of the country in a story about Bishop's mother worrying about not seeing her son while he was under house arrest and subsequently about getting information about the whereabouts of his body after he was killed—this from a paper that made a policy decision "not to carry a word Bishop had to say when he came here only three months ago as Prime Minister of his country to attend the Caricom Heads of Government conference." He then went on to remind readers that "it was Bishop who led the regime that made those 'murderers' into what they are today. It was he who led the militarization of Grenadian society to the point where army generals and colonels became ambassadors in high places and held high rank in the central committee of the NJM party."

But it was an editorial by the *Guardian* that most disturbed Trinidad's government. It was a savage personal attack on the Trinidad prime minister, Mr. George Chambers. Because it was such an uncharacteristic departure from the normal tone of the paper, it highlighted the strong emotions felt by all who had anything to do with the Grenada affair.

We think the entire Caricom family must extend the most sincere thanks to the Organization of Eastern Caribbean States and, in particular, to the Prime Minister of St. Lucia, who insisted from the start that only strong intervention in Grenada could have any effect. . . .

We should all further extend thanks to the Prime Minister of Barbados. . . .

As chilling events have shown beyond any kind of doubt Grenada had become the arsenal of Communist hemispheric ambitions.

With Trinidad and Tobago only 90 miles away from Grenada and a gang of murderous men in power there, what guarantee was there that we could have escaped their criminal intentions, if their insane strategy impelled them?

In these circumstances, we think the decisive manner in which the President of the United States acted in directing American troops to go to Grenada and intervene is also not only commendable but it has turned out to be an action that has saved innumerable Caricom lives and has given infinite hope that never again will the threat of Communist domination grab us by the throat. . . .

Mr. Chambers, our Prime Minister, has demonstrated several unsatisfactory traits of leadership: indecision, ignorance of military affairs, poor knowledge of the psychology of Communists and their stooges, and worse, appalling ignorance of what public opinion in this country really thinks of armed intervention in Grenada by the United States. . . .

With a mammoth arsenal behind him, with Cubans who have lived up to the challenge of Fidel Castro to die for the revolution, out of pique or coercion or sheer bravado, Gen. Hudson Austin would have refused any such request and gone about his business enslaving his own people and thumbing his nose at us. . . .

What the events of this week have shown us is that we are too far behind in military technology, diplomatic skills and political psychology to do much at this stage and be more than a burden to others in the global conflict unfolding. . . .

Gratitude for American intervention pervades the streets and there is a discernible acknowledgement that the Cubans have been putting up one titanic struggle that the ordinary man here had not thought possible—"against the Americans" at that. . . .

Our people truly deserve more sagacious and decisive leadership, committed to total defence of the common heritage of democracy which we share with the U.S.[7]

The editorial itself was a stinging below to a prime minister who had been in office for only two and a half years, following some twenty years of rule by the founder and leader since independence, Dr. Eric Williams. To follow in the footsteps of a legend is a most difficult task, and to avoid negative comparison is nearly impossible. It was these circumstances that seemed to cause the government of Trinidad to react strongly to the events following the invasion within the Caricom group and that eventually led to a war of words between Trinidad on one side and Barbados and some of her Caribbean neighbors on the other.

The position of the government of Barbados, one of the prime movers behind the invasion, was best articulated by its prime minister, J. G. M. Adams. Mr. Adams, after winning two successive election campaigns and steering his tourist-dependent island into economic buoyancy through a serious world recession and an even more serious Third World recession, had earned a reputation as an extremely able administrator and economic manager. Both at home and within the Eastern Caribbean area he had built himself a reputation as a tough politician, independent minded and determined to do what was necessary to preserve political stability in the ministates, for which Barbados is a leader. The lack of flamboyance of his politics and the relatively small area of his influence has obscured a man of tremendous talent, will, and determination, who refuses to play to the gallery within the Caribbean and world arena or to overextend his reach and that which his country's economy could sustain. While he might not get the endorsement of some activist political groups, his actions provide a lubricant for them to survive. In an interview he responded to the ruckus being raised internationally over the U.S.-led invasion.

I think many of the countries lack an understanding of the peculiarly close relationship that exists between West Indians. Countries are criticising not so much the Caribbean States, but the United States for participating in an act which had overwhelming popular support in those countries which had a consensus the like of which perhaps no European country or the United States has enjoyed on any issue since the Second World War.

They can't see that the Third World is not homogeneous; that military government and non-democratic government was and is a grave affront to the people of the Caribbean. That those Caribbean states who have departed from democracy, Commonwealth Caribbean states I speak of, are resented and disliked in the rest of the Caribbean and that even Bishop, God rest his memory, is only tolerated in the rest of the Caribbean. His pattern was not thought of to be one which the rest of us would want to follow.

And some weight could have been given by the countries which are critical to the sense of unity which West Indians feel and the sense of outrage which at all levels, except apparently in Guyana, we felt when a Prime Minister and half of his Cabinet was massacred.

On the other hand . . . you cannot expect every country in the world to show a total sensitivity for the problems of very small islands far away. There may be many countries in the world who do not wish a precedent to be set . . . allowing the United States or Soviet Union, the two superpowers, to intervene at their own convenience in the internal affairs of other countries.

I think that we must argue and explain that first of all the intervention was legal, although legalistic talk may not get you very far in this world. Secondly, we must explain that the situation, although not totally unique, is simply not applicable to the great majority of trouble spots in the world.

I am suggesting that the Eastern Caribbean, on entirely a different level, is also a situation which has its own rules. The feeling among people in the Eastern Caribbean is such that we should be understood and given the benefit of any conceivable doubts that could remain, and the final point I make which relates to the United States is that now that we know what was in Grenada and suspected all along, it would have been quite impossible for the West Indies, even if we raised all the military forces available—the Jamaican army, the Trinidad army, all the small island special service units, Barbados army, the Army of Belize and the Bahamas, we would not have been able to undertake an operation in Grenada with any success.[8]

In his island nation of Barbados, Prime Minister Adams enjoyed overwhelming support for the action he took in coordinating the strategy of the nations participating in the invasion. One editorial gave this assessment of the situation Barbados faced and of Adams's response:

It had to be done. There was no way that the small nations of the Eastern Caribbean in particular, could hope to rest comfortably after events took an unexpectedly brutal turn in Grenada over the past few days unless action was taken against the ruthless military regime there. It could not have been an easy decision to make to send armed contingents into Grenada. Those facing it would have known only too well that there would be talk about infringement of the sovereignty of Grenada, a principle that many have shown a preparedness to latch on to when it suits them to perpetuate their dastardly act. . . . It is folly to mouth high-sounding principles when it is obvious that those involved have no regard for common humanity.

After asking what had been done to enable the Grenadian people to "recapture their true sovereignty as people," having gone from one autocratic government to another, the editorial noted:

The Barbados Government under Mr. Tom Adams has figured in the decision to go into Grenada. It was not an action for timid hearts nor one of callous indifference. If anything, it was prompted by the callous disregard for human life which Austin and his minions established from early in their lust for power.

Now it is time for Barbadians, who all along were crying out for something to be done, to help improve the Grenada situation and to rally around their leadership. Much of what was said after the recent executions in Grenada showed that we are still a people of conscience. This is not the time for us to allow our detractors to weaken our resolve.[9]

But there were some voices raised within Barbados who totally disagreed with the decision of the Barbados government and others to invade. The editor of the *Caribbean Contact* condemned the invasion and labelled it unjustifiable on any "legal or moral ground." He called the invasion "a dangerous precedent" and predicted that it would have "far-reaching implications for the future peace and security of the entire Caribbean." He reiterated the Reagan administration's long struggle to subvert the Bishop government and his anxiety over the U.S. government's practice of disseminating unsubstantiated reports to bolster its position when a less confrontational path could have been taken. The editor, Ricky Singh, went on to say of the invasion: "The Cuban statement disassociating the Castro government from any involvement in the leadership struggle within the NJM, and its own position to take a neutral stand, at first robbed the United States–inspired propaganda machinery of some fuel. It later perhaps influenced the decision to invade while Cuba was still determining what, if any, involvement should there be on the side of the Grenadian people, among whom were over 300 of its own citizens, most of them workers at the new airport site."[10] Except for this, however, the prime minister of Barbados enjoyed nearly unanimous support for his actions within his island nation.

When Prime Minister Eugenia Charles of Dominica arrived home after flying to the United States to lend support to the Reagan administration and to put the OECS case to the world, she was given a grand welcome home by a large crowd at the airport.[11] The Caribbean papers had given her able defense of the invasion full prominence as she went from conference to conference. Though coming relatively late into active politics, she had proved herself at home and abroad to be an intelligent, resourceful, and tough politician who, once she took a position, worked systematically to see it through to the end.

The government of Prime Minister Edward Seaga of Jamaica took part eagerly in the U.S.-led invasion. Seaga's Jamaica Labour Party (JLP) had come to power in 1980 after advocating a return to free enterprise and a turn away from ten years of democratic socialist rule by Michael Manley and his People's National Party (PNP). Because Manley had been a close friend of Fidel Castro and Maurice Bishop, the relatively new Reagan administration took a strong interest in the Jamaica election and made it obvious that it preferred Seaga to win. Following his victory, Seaga kindled a strong friendship with the Reagan administration, which tried to arrange all help within its means to aid Jamaica, while pushing the free enterprise model on which they both agreed ideologically as suitable for developing nations. Within the Caribbean, at Caricom heads of government meetings, Prime Minister Seaga from the time he took office attacked the presence of undemocratic Grenada among their number. However, the other Caribbean leaders prevailed upon both Seaga and Bishop to moderate their positions.

Seaga's link with violent party gangs had always been troubling even for some within his party. Before his election as prime minister some observers wondered in private whether once in office Edward Seaga would treat the opposition as fairly in the elections as he had been by the democratic socialist government of Michael Manley. The similarity in the way both the U.S. government and Seaga viewed the Bishop government was prompted by the JLP's traditional anticommunist stand, its opposition to Manley's socialist experiment in the preceding years, and Bishop's close association with Cuba and Jamaica. Prime Minister Seaga's decision to participate in the U.S.-led invasion was supported by 56 percent of the Jamaican electorate.[12] This solid support was based on a strong anticommunist sentiment within the JLP constituency and on Bishop's popularity among the PNP headed by Manley. "The majority of Jamaicans saw the invasion as a rescue mission. They identified with this act of aggression designed to teach communist activists a political lesson. They empathized with the rationale which suggested that the Revolutionary Military Council which replaced Bishop was a threat to peace and stability in the Caribbean."[13]

Like the other Caribbean governments, Jamaica had followed the unfolding events in Grenada with interest. As soon as news of Bishop's death reached Jamaica, Prime Minister Seaga determined to take action. On October 20, 1983, he summoned an emergency cabinet meeting. In a nationwide broadcast that evening the prime minister gave his views on the Grenada situation. After expressing his disgust at the tragic news from Grenada, he went on to paint a grim picture of the Soviet-Cuban direction in which Bishop and his colleagues were leading their nation.

Nor did it surprise us to learn that the means by which he was overthrown was violent, since it is one of the basic principles of communism that the means of change is by violent revolution.

What, however, did surprise us was the intensity of the barbarity by which the change of leadership in Grenada was accomplished.

It was a dark and dishonorable day for those who have now taken over the Government of Grenada, it was a dark day for all of us in the English-speaking Caribbean. We have witnessed a new and sinister development which is totally inimical to the values of the rest of the Caribbean community, and to the democratic traditions to which we subscribe.

Jamaica has been warning about the dangers inherent in the system of Government introduced and enforced by Mr. Bishop in 1979, in Grenada, when he himself led the revolution which was never subsequently legitimized by the Grenadian people through the electoral process.

The brutality of what happened in Grenada yesterday brings into sharp relief the two systems that exist within the Caribbean area—systems which have different methods and procedures for changing governments and leaders: The democratic system by the ballot, and the totalitarian system by the bullet.[14]

The preliminary explanation was an excellent summation of the view of most Jamaicans while also interjecting the particular anticommunist bent of Prime Minister Seaga and his Jamaican Labour Party. The opposition People's National Party, headed by Michael Manley, condemned the Revolutionary Military Council for its acts of violence against Bishop and his colleagues, but disagreed strongly with any type of intervention. They saw developments in Grenada as purely an internal matter that could be resolved by the Caricom states through economic and diplomatic pressure.

But Prime Minister Seaga gave his best analysis and defense of the Grenada situation and of the invasion after he returned from the Caricom conference and after the invasion was under way. In a report to "Parliament and the Nation," he analyzed the Grenada situation was follows:

The seeds of this tragic situation were sown five years ago when the corrupt Government of Eric Gairy was overthrown by a coup led by Mr. Maurice Bishop. While there was no question that the Gairy administration had forfeited the respect of all decent citizens of the Caribbean, this Government, which was then in opposition, from the outset took the view that a dangerous precedent had been set which would inevitably have disastrous consequences. I urged at that time that recognition of the Bishop regime should be withheld until it secured a mandate from the electorate. This would make certain, I said then, that the principle of armed overthrow of a Government is not accepted in the Commonwealth Caribbean, and would reinforce the electoral system as the only recognized basis of selecting a government. From the outset this administration viewed the establishment of a Government by coup in Grenada in 1979 as having far-reaching implications for the future of the democratic process on which all the Governments of this region are based. . . . It may be felt that these matters do not concern us, but most certainly they do. If a whole Government can be wiped out overnight by political or military extremists and the Governments of the Caribbean remain silent and passive, then no Government elected by the people can be safe from madmen of one type or another who would seek to replace a government of the people, elected by the people with one selected by a chosen few or whatever nature.

If we ignore the occurrence of brutal military take-over or political overthrows of governments, we would immediately give heart to every subversive group within the region to engineer disorder and instability as a means of overthrow. No democratic system of government would have a chance of carrying out the programmes of development which it was elected to implement if in its midst was a group of subversives, anarchists and terrorists bent on destruction of the foundations of stability which under-pin the whole system of democracy. The far-reaching consequences of such neglect on our part would be awesome, and would have the effect of creating an unsure and unsecure future for all of us.

Prime Minister Seaga went on to state the intentions of the Caribbean leaders then and for the future: "Today's Caribbean leadership is determined that instances of military and revolutionary take-overs must be dealt with in such a manner as will leave no room for doubt whatsoever as to the will of the majority of the English-speaking Caribbean."

Having said that, Seaga painted Grenada as posing a subversive threat to her fragile neighbors by providing military training for some groups, maintaining a large, overproportionate army, and using its powerful radio transmitters for propaganda purposes. He then gave his analysis and perception of the threat and how it had changed with Bishop's death:

While Maurice Bishop was alive there was some indication that these capabilities could and would be used in this subversive manner against neighboring states as there were complaints regarding training of a para-military and military nature taking place in Grenada among citizens of neighboring countries known for their own subversive interests.

However, whatever may have been the threat, it was minimal in the hands of Maurice Bishop, who was a moderate in comparison with the military and political leaders of the regime which overthrew him.

A totally different picture emerges when this array of military and subversive capability came to be at the disposal of one of the most extremist groups of men to assume control of any country in recent time. Few countries can have claimed the experience of having its entire Cabinet wiped out in the manner in which that of Grenada was exterminated.

Who then can blame the Eastern Caribbean States for perceiving this combination of awesome might and brutal men, who apparently had no concept of where to stop in taking human life, as a prelude to hostile action being taken, beyond their own borders by those in power in Grenada.[15]

His was a reasoned, skillful, and forceful presentation as to why they had mounted the invasion and a statement of the rules of those participating in the invasion.

Thus, while President Reagan and his administration were being buffeted, at home and around the world, by severe criticism of their action, the majority of people and their governments in the Caribbean were solidly behind the invasion. However, at the other end of the Caribbean, Guyana, which had in the Caricom conference argued forcefully against any type of military intervention, perhaps fearing that a similar decision would be made against it in the future, and had proposed that the crisis be dealt with through political, diplomatic, and economic means, continued a war of words against those states that participated in the invasion. The administration of President Forbes Burnham not only cosponsored the UN resolution that condemned the invasion action, but Burnham personally mounted an offensive against some Caricom leaders.

Although there is no way of gauging the reaction of the press and people of Guyana to the invasion independent of the government's position, conversations with some citizens and government officials suggest stronger support for the invasion than the government or its controlled press might like to admit. President Burnham, once the darling of much of the Caribbean, had in recent years become more of an odd man out in Caribbean affairs as his promising economic and political experiments of the seventies collapsed in the face of the oil shocks, recession, and mismanagement. His determination to hold on to power through a series of machinations, including the severe repression of most of his political foes, caused a further deterioration of his image in the area. His flamboyant style and political pontifications at home and on the international stage in the face of his country's near bankruptcy had engendered much disrespect for him and his priorities. His opposition, therefore, though noted, was not treated seriously by many of his Caribbean colleagues.

Despite this, Guyana, like Jamaica, Belize, and the Bahamas, is an integral part of the Caricom alliance. In the light of the past experience of a failed Caribbean Federation, it behooves all of the leaders, especially the victorious Adams and Seaga, to come to terms with those leaders who were not totally pleased with their leading roles in the invasion. The way they resolve the internal tensions caused by the invasion will ultimately determine their statesmanship, reveal their true talents and leadership ability, and determine the future of the valuable Caricom.

In looking at the reasons given for mounting the invasion, one must ask (1) did Prime Minister Adams and the OECS heads of state actually believe that there was a threat to their security, and (2) was their belief reasonable? In the first instance the heads of state did actually believe that Grenada posed a threat to their security, as they told the British parliamentary commission a year prior to the invasion. But even a sympathetic view of their position suggests that there was no real threat. Rather, Prime Minister Adams and the OECS heads of state showed by their action that they had accepted the American political belief that, regardless of the facts, sees every radical as a Communist. It is their form of reactive thinking that allowed a segment of the West Indian population in general and the Grenadian population in particular to support the invasion. This is why the people on the island of Carriacou, who praised the Bishop government for sending them their first dentist, rejected his services and his presence once the invasion was completed because he was Cuban even though they readily admit that he was completely apolitical and refused to give a political reaction even when goaded.

It is this attitude that the left wing in the Caribbean sees as an automatic reflex where people neglect their interests and fight other people's battles. They see West Indians as more worried about the alleged plan of Communists to enslave the world than about the fact that the governments who preach about this conspiracy to them were until recently their real enslavers and still support the current enslavers of their brothers in South Africa.

While the support Reagan got from the governments and people of the Caribbean was heartening to the administration, the indications of how the Grenadians themselves felt took a while longer. When the news came a few weeks later, it was an apparent vindication for his action and policy: 86 percent of the population favored intervention, while only 9 percent were opposed.

If, as has been suggested, the positive attitude toward the United States in the Commonwealth Caribbean is due to the administration of the people of the area for the great economic strides made by the people of the United States and the migration of millions of Caribbean people to the United States, then one must ask why the same is not true for Latin America, where relatively the same situation exists. The only explanation seems to be that while the Latin Americans have had a long history of United States interventions that only succeeded in replacing one oligarchy with another, the Commonwealth Caribbean, until recently under the control of the British, remained relatively isolated from these events. As a result, the politicians and people of the Commonwealth Caribbean seemed not to attach as much weight to the implications of their action or may have been self-confident enough to feel that they could themselves deal with the situation through their own regional mechanism once the invasion was over.

NOTES

1. "Trinidadians Solidly behind the Invasion," *Trinidad Sunday Express*, October 30, 1983.

2. Karl Hudson-Phillips, "Invasion was Justified," *Trinidad Sunday Express*, October 30, 1983.

3. Ibid.

4. Patrick Solomon, "A Most Insulting Lack of Faith," *Trinidad Sunday Express*, October 30, 1983.

5. "Campus Comes Out against Invasion," *Trinidad Sunday Express*, October 30, 1983.

6. Andy Johnson, "Crocodile Tears and Betrayal of a Principle," *Trinidad Sunday Express*, October 30, 1983.

7. "Shocking Ineptness by Trinidad," *Trinidad Guardian*, October 29, 1983.

8. Ken Gordon, "We Have Our Own Rules in the Caribbean—JGM Adams" (interview), *Trinidad Sunday Express*, October 30, 1983.

9. Editorial, "The Die is Cast," *Barbados Advocate*, October 26, 1983.

10. *Barbados Nation*, October 28, 1983.

11. *Barbados Nation*, October 26, 1983.

12. Carl Stone, "The Jamaican Reaction, Grenada and the Political Stalemate," *Caribbean Review* 12, no. 4 (Fall 1983):61.

13. Ibid.

14. *Jamaica Gleaner*, October 21, 1983.

15. Edward Seaga, "Statement to the Nation by the Prime Minister of Jamaica," *Information Service*, October 26, 1983.

7

Trouble in the Periphery: British Reaction to the Invasion

Even though the main event of the U.S.-Caribbean invasion was centered in Washington and in Caribbean areas, an important development was occurring in Great Britain as well. As the former "mother country" of the Commonwealth Caribbean nations, Britain still wields enormous influence and prestige in the area. Its continuing financial, economic, social, and cultural relations are still of great importance to both sides, though a deliberate attempt has been made over the last two decades to diversify the dependent relationship of the past and to substitute this with one of greater independence and self-interest. The former colonial relationship gave Britain a special status and a close familiarity with many of the actors of the area. Partly as a result of this relationship, the British press coverage of the events in the area began earlier and reflected a more general, international perspective.

On October 22, 1983, the London *Times* reported the Caribbean response to the murder of Maurice Bishop and four members of his cabinet in a front-page article. The reporters noted the actions each government had taken or was expected to take and the preparations being made for the OECS and Caricom heads of government conferences. The reporters also noted Cuba's reaction to the death of Bishop and his colleagues: Cuba had declared three days of national mourning for their deaths, saying, "No doctrine, no principle nor position proclaimed as revolutionary—and no internal division—can justify savage methods such as the elimination of Maurice Bishop and the outstanding group of honest and moral leaders who died."[1]

When the United States diverted its task force en route to Lebanon to the Caribbean, the British also moved HMS *Antrim*, a guided-missile destroyer located within two days of the area on the Colombian coast, so that it could be used to evacuate the 350 British citizens on Grenada should the situation continue to deteriorate and the United States decide to evacuate its citizens. Following President Reagan's announcement to the world that the U.S.-led invasion of Grenada was under way, British politicians demanded answers from their government. In a heated session of Parliament, Prime Minister Margaret Thatcher said that she had indicated to the U.S. government her very considerable doubts about initiating action in Grenada.[2] Later the United States indicated to the British government that the view taken by the Caribbean states had weighed heavily and conclusively in the decision to intervene. But members of Parliament were dissatisfied by the discrepancies between the British government's own view of the situation and that of the U.S. and Caribbean leaders, with whom they had a close relationship. While Lady Janet Young, minister of state and commonwealth affairs, was telling the House of Lords that "the Grenada Government was putting no difficulties in the way of those wishing to leave the island,"[3] and Sir Geoffrey Howe, the secretary of state for foreign affairs, was saying that he had no reason to think that American military intervention was likely and that he knew of no American intention to invade Grenada, contradictory facts emerged the next day.[4]

The Reagan administration's actions in seeking the British government's advice in the first instance, then returning within hours of the actual invasion to announce that the United States indeed intended to go ahead, struck many British politicians as shocking, given their government's own assessment of the problem. Members of Parliament therefore sought a debate on the subject. But while the British government had been looking at the situation as a Grenadian problem, the United States was looking at it in geopolitical terms, and the Caribbean leaders were doing so in regional terms. The difference in perspective eventually dictated the response of each, but the stage had been set for a cantankerous debate after the shadow foreign secretary of the Labour party, Mr. Denis Healey, demanded that the prime minister and foreign secretary protest directly to the United States in the strongest possible terms about the invasion. He termed the foreign secretary's lack of knowledge about the invasion "an extraordinary statement to come from a representative of a Government which prides itself on being America's most loyal ally.'' He then went on to say: ''It appears from what the Foreign Secretary has to tell us that the British Government has on this occasion been deceived by its American ally and by some of its Commonwealth partners.'' He further stated that the American decision had ''already split Commonwealth States in the Caribbean and represents an unpardonable humiliation.'' Mr. Healey concluded his main retorts by saying: ''It must appear to any reasonable person that the excuse given by the U.S. government in this matter was dishonest—I must use that word—and that this was a conspiracy by a number of governments to invade an independent part of the British Commonwealth for which no excuses can be given, and I am glad to say the Foreign Secretary has offered none.'' While an obvious play to the gallery was intended by Mr. Healey's remarks, there was serious concern among many that the British government was either badly informed or misled, hence the need for a full debate. It was also an attempt to show up the government as being inept and uninformed about the intentions of its staunch ally, the United States.

Britain had been issued an invitation to join the OECS and its partners in the Grenada invasion at 7 P.M. on Monday, October 24. The invitation was delivered to the British High Commissioner in Barbados for transmittal to London, despite the fact that British opposition and skepticism were known. Nevertheless, a formal invitation was made because the OECS leaders felt that Britain still could play a role in the whole affair. Prior to the issuance of the official invitation, the British government was sounded out as a possible invasion partner, so the British diplomats knew on Friday, October 21, that this was the ultimate intention of the OECS. The invitation was declined, according to the British government, because of a fear for British lives and particularly that of the governor general, Sir Paul Scoon, as representative of the queen.[5] The United States, after being sounded out as a possible partner by Sunday, October 23, flew a high-ranking military officer to Barbados to begin military coordination and so that Washington could have direct contact with Caribbean developments.

Britain handled the event and its developments as routine. From the outset the British government adopted this attitude because it knew that the Caribbean islands did not have the material to undertake such a task by themselves. Having reached that conclusion, British officials did not think that the United States would go ahead with such a delicate operation in a Commonwealth country without informing them and giving their view serious consideration. As a consequence, the maneuvers by the OECS countries and their partners, Barbados and Jamaica, were missed over the weekend, leading to serious misunderstandings with the United States.

When President Reagan called Mrs. Thatcher on Monday, October 24, to say that he was giving serious consideration to the request and added that he would let her know in advance of any decision that was made, plans for the actual invasion were already far advanced. This was necessary because the logistical preparations had to be made by the planners so as to accommodate any final decision by the president. President Reagan, because he was not himself involved in the discussions and planning sessions, was in no position in a telephone conversation to give Mrs. Thatcher any more than the barest information. The element of surprise also necessitated that as little time as possible elapse between the order to proceed and the actual engagement. So when President Reagan called Mrs. Thatcher again to announce his final decision to respond to the request, the first message was still being considered at Downing Street.

In the House of Commons debate the opposition sensed that the government was on the defensive and prepared to make the most of it. Foreign Secretary Sir Geoffrey Howe, in a detailed presentation of the government's dealings with Washington before the invasion of Grenada, admitted that consultations by the U.S. administration were "regrettably" less than the British ministers would have liked.[6] Dr. David Owen of the Social Democrats tried to force Secretary Howe to admit that the invasion was a breach of the United Nations Charter, but this, to the annoyance of the opposition, Sir Geoffrey would not do. Mr. Denis Healey, after several severe attacks on the government, accused the secretary of servility in his dealings with the Americans.

While the government could afford to rely on its majority, there was some dissension in the ranks. The most telling was the accusation made by Mr. Julian Amery, who said that the government could either have taken a stand against American intervention or have gone into it wholeheartedly, as he himself would have wished, but they had lapsed into "a pallid abstention."[7] While the government survived the vote by 336 to 221, the debate showed the government to be inept, uninformed, and very closely dependent on U.S. policy in this matter. The opposition skillfully worked to link the law-and-order Mrs. Thatcher with President Reagan, whose actions in Grenada they saw as contrary to international law and the United Nations Charter. Its attempt to show the United States as in some way deceiving and untrustworthy was clearly aimed at appealing to the growing nuclear freeze movement in Britain, which opposed Thatcher's position. Although the government won the debate, the opposition had clearly created enough speculation about and opposition to the government's stance in this matter to shake its confidence.

The opposition kept prodding the government with question after question. Then in the government's own ranks dissent arose: "A motion explicitly approving the intervention by the United States and its Caribbean partners, and by implication criticizing the government, was tabled in the Commons with two former ministers, Mr. Geoffrey Rippon and Mr. Howell, among the sponsors."[8] At a closed meeting of some members of its back bench, the government was accused by another former minister, Sir Hugh Fraser, of being politically inept in deciding to hold a debate the following Monday on the deployment of cruise and Pershing II missiles. While he admitted that the debate was necessary, he thought that it was foolish to hold it at a time of increasing mistrust over U.S. intentions.[9] With dissent in the government's ranks growing, the opposition felt confident in increasing its pressure on the government. Labour leader Mr. Neil Kinnock sought at question time to provoke Mrs. Thatcher by asking the prime minister what obligation she then felt for Mr. Reagan. In a confident and forceful reply, Mrs. Thatcher responded: "The obligations of a very close ally without whose support freedom and justice in Europe would be in doubt."[10] Her party erupted with cheers of support for her strong and loyal statement as she took her seat after answering. But Mr. Kinnock, none the worse for his bruising, unabashedly suggested that the "special relationship" had turned out to be not so special and invited the prime minister, "in the chaos and humiliation of the Grenada affair," to demonstrate greater independence in furthering British interests.[11]

The Conservative Thatcher government, slowly sinking in a morass of questions and taunting from the opposition, and to a lesser extent from its own backbenchers, was under great pressure to make a clear statement of policy on the whole Grenada affair. This came on October 30. Before the official response, Foreign Secretary Sir Geoffrey Howe gave an indication that the government had drastically revised its position when he admitted that the British government had complained to the American government about the lack of frankness over its invasion plans. The United States, he said, had not given Britain "an opportunity of consultations in those last crucial stages of the kind we would have wished."[12] Sir Geoffrey also admitted that the invasion was not justified on the grounds of danger to American citizens or of Cuban-Soviet presence. He said that "Cubans or Russians could be discovered in many other parts of the world, but if they were in those countries as a result of an invitation, however misguided of the governments concerned, that did not provide a justification for invasion."[13]

But it was Mrs. Thatcher's statement on October 30 that clinched the government's shift of position. In an address on national radio about Anglo-American relations after the invasion of Grenada, she said: "If we are going to pronounce a new law that whenever Communism reigns against the will of people . . . the United States shall enter, then we are going to have really terrible wars in the world." After expressing her delight that the people of Grenada were free and that the people of the Eastern Caribbean could sleep more soundly in their beds, she went on to add: "Does this mean you are entitled to go into a whole list of other countries? I think the answer is no."[14] While Mrs. Thatcher's statement was in keeping with her ideological positions, it seems clear that she was forced to air her differences with Washington publicly because of opposition pressure, which probably could have caused a spillover into other foreign policy areas. Her statement came shortly before the House of Commons was due to debate the deployment of cruise missiles "amid growing evidence of public mistrust, in the aftermath of the Grenada invasion, of the American guarantee of joint U.S.-British control over the firing of the missiles."[15] The episode showed the extent of the direct influence of U.S. policy in a rather remote area.

While the Grenada incident died a slow death in the public debate, the House of Commons Foreign Affairs Committee decided that the matter warranted further study to elicit and analyze more calmly British policy toward Grenada and determine why an apparent breakdown of such major proportions occurred between Britain and her Commonwealth partners in the Caribbean. The committee's report noted with some pride, and relief, that the committee was welcomed as friends throughout its visit and in "particular by all those we met, formally, or informally, in Grenada."[16] The report began by reviewing the findings and recommendations of a report done a year earlier, which had recommended that the United Kingdom should "work to promote a dialogue with the government of Grenada," strengthen its representation in Grenada, and not turn its back on further aid, particularly in the field of legal resources. The report went on to observe that the government's response to this recommendation "did not in our view indicate sufficient recognition of the potentially critical nature of the situation in Grenada and the need for positive policies to provide an effective antidote to Cuban and Soviet influence in the island."[17]

This attitude by the Thatcher government toward Grenada was a direct result of its staunch and often unquestioning support for the policies of the Reagan administration. It was an abrogation of its own responsibility to a Commonwealth nation and showed a preference instead to link its foreign policy to that of the Reagan administration. That Her Majesty's government, with over 400 years of colonial experience, could yield so easily on a purely political issue is astonishing. After recapping the domestic dynamics of Grenada's society under Maurice Bishop and the New Jewel Movement, the report went onto analyze how Grenada's foreign policy came to take the sharp turn that it did.

The movement towards alignment with Cuba and the Eastern bloc countries was encouraged by the decision of many Western bloc countries to limit diplomatic relations and bilateral aid and assistance agreements with Grenada until the constitutional position was regularized, although some multilateral aid, including European Community aid, continued to flow throughout the period of Revolutionary Government. The United Kingdom, for example, continued to honor its commitments under the 1974 Aid Settlement following independence, but entered into no new aid agreements after the overthrow of the Gairy regime. Like most Western powers, however, the United Kingdom neither broke off diplomatic relations with Grenada nor prevented strictly commercial transactions between the United Kingdom and public and private enterprise in Grenada.

A result of this drawback of assistance by Western bloc countries was the creation of a vacuum only too easily filled by Cuba, the Soviet Union and Soviet allies. In October 1979 Cuba agreed to provide major assistance in the form of equipment, materials and construction workers towards the construction of the new international airport at Point Salines, a project also supported by loans and grants from Venezuela, Libya, Algeria and O.P.E.C., and by substantial tax levies on the Grenadian people.[18]

The passage quoted above more than anything else shows the extent to which the policies of the Thatcher government toward Grenada mirrored those of the United States. It also shows the difficulty a small country can encounter once the United States makes its displeasure with that country known. But it also points to a more fundamental problem in the international system. It shows the extent to which middle powers like Britain, rather than seeing a role for themselves in the international system as adviser and conciliator, have taken a back seat, thus allowing potentially small and avoidable confrontations to escalate into super-power rivalry. It may well be that it is this lack of will in former great nations to see the positive role that they can play in international affairs, independent of the United States, that has in part led to greater instability in the international system. If anyone was in a suitable position to play a part in the Grenada affair long before it reached the point of crisis, Britain was. With the inaction of middle powers, every confrontation is allowed to escalate until the superpowers or their surrogates enter the picture, whereupon the affair is acted out as a full-blown international crisis. It is an inherently dangerous way for the world to conduct its affairs. As the House of Commons report noted: "Events in Grenada have, therefore, provided further evidence of the vulnerability of small states to external pressure, and at the same time have demonstrated the susceptibility of apparently stable international alliances and communities to the disruptive effects of events on their margins. As the world has so often learned in the past, and at such great cost, wars break out, and alliances fall apart, not so often as the result of deliberate decisions by the major powers, but as a result of the inability of the great power system, and the alliances which support it, to cope with the problems of small countries in far away parts of the globe."[19]

One year prior to the Grenada invasion, the first House of Commons report had noted what it saw as a "clear wish by many political leaders in the West Indies for the United Kingdom to make a more positive and distinctive approach to the region and particularly CARICOM states." Little wonder, then, that until the very end the OECS and its partners in the invasion were hoping that the British government would heed their concern. But while Britain waited on a promised invitation and pondered legal and constitutional details, her former colonies persuaded the United States to act. When the actions of President Reagan, the leaders of the Caribbean states, and the United Kingdom government in the whole episode are considered, one can only conclude that some leaders make things happen, some watch things happen, and others just simply ask what has happened as events pass them by. Mention has been made that the British government may have been reluctant to act on the Caribbean request because of how this might have looked to her other Commonwealth partners. This may well have been so, but it could also be bureaucratic justification for the lack of a clear policy and the will to lead. For not only did Britain possess a mother-country relationship that she could have used, but she also had the Commonwealth office through which she could have acted to thrash out the legal and political complications she might have had to face had she decided to act. It seems clear that Britain missed many opportunities to use diplomacy in the beginning and failed to support the very principles for which it often proclaims that it stands in the end. In the Caribbean the saying is "taking other people's eyes to see."

NOTES

1. Jeremy Taylor and Christopher Thomas, "Cuba Condemns Grenada and Jamaica Severs Relations," *The Times*, (London) October 22, 1983, p. 1.

2. "Government Warned President over Action in Caribbean," *The Times*, October 26, 1983, p. 4.

3. Ibid.

4. Ibid.

5. Henry Stanhope, "Britain Refuses Offer to Join Grenada Invasion," *The Times*, October 26, 1983, p. 6.

6. Julian Haviland, "Howe Refuses to Condemn Reagan," *The Times*, October 27, 1983, p. 1.

7. Ibid.

8. Ibid.

9. Julian Haviland, "Tory Gloom Grows over Invasion," *The Times*, October 28, 1983, p. 1.

10. Ibid.

11. Philip Webster, "Thatcher Comes off the Fence," *The Times*, October 31, 1983, p. 1.

12. Ibid.

13. Ibid.

14. Ibid.

15. Ibid.

16. House of Commons, Foreign Affairs Committee, Second Report from Grenada, Session 1983–84, March 1984, p. v.

17. Ibid., p. vi.

18. Ibid., p. vii.

19. Ibid., p. xxxix.

8

U.S. Foreign Policy Decision Making Leading to Grenada

Few administrations have been elected with a clearer pledge to restore U.S. credibility and greatness abroad than the Reagan administration. Events prior to and especially during the Carter administration had contributed to an almost unanimous call by Americans for a more assertive foreign policy. During the Carter administration U.S.-Soviet relations reached such an impasse that the Senate refused to ratify the SALT II agreement. Critics charged that SALT II gave the Russians a decisively unfair advantage. U.S. clandestine operations had failed to install a pro-Western government in Angola as the Cuban/Soviet–backed party led the country into independence. In addition, the numerous revelations of CIA excesses both at home and abroad helped to sully its reputation, bringing it under closer congressional scrutiny and curtailing some of its activity. In Nicaragua U.S. influence failed to install a moderate government; instead the Cuban-backed guerrillas emerged dominant. Then there was the Soviet invasion of Afghanistan, a case of naked aggression, where the Soviets installed a government of their choice and then proceeded to fight a war against an indigenous resistance movement.

These "losses" and perceived concessions to the Soviets were seen as caused by the Carter administration's lack of competence and its failure to understand the Soviets and their desire for world domination. This view or some version of it dominated the thinking and argument of the political Right and soon came to influence that of many moderates as well. President Carter put his prestige on the line when he sought Senate approval for the return of the Panama Canal to the government of that country. It was a heated debate that saw, as most such debates do, a number of big-stick senators from what used to be called the "acreage states" featured as prominent opponents. As one of these senators reminded the president during the debate, "We stole it fair and square." Although he won narrow passage of the treaty, the fight left President Carter vulnerable and the political Right suspicious of his handling of foreign policy matters. The Iran hostage crisis was another embarrassment, not only for the Carter presidency but for the people of the United States as well. Although it may have been handled badly at the start, with the president passionately committing himself to obtaining the hostages' release, it was largely not a situation of his making. However, his commitment, the attendant publicity in the media, and the protracted duration of the crisis eventually did in his administration. His detractors laid these problems squarely at his door. Because the domestic economy under his stewardship saw high inflation, a drop in productivity, and a flotilla of illegal immigrants from Cuba and Haiti, the American people got the impression of an administration in disarray, being led by events rather than leading.

Carter had sold himself to the people not as a man of ideals, as Kennedy did, or as a motivator, as Roosevelt did, but as a manager who could fix the very problems that were already beginning to surface; but when Carter turned his attention to a number of less pressing problems, even his supporters thought that it was a wrong ordering of priorities. When the unanticipated problems arrived upon the now mushrooming original ones, his administration faltered. While Carter was beleaguered from all sides, superficial explanations were offered by entrenched interests for the country's problems. After more than a decade of upheaval and change, the country longed for less exciting times and a chance to reassess the recent past. It was easy for Carter's detractors to obscure the progress and successes of his administration.

Restoring America's credibility, according to the Reagan administration, seemed to mean (1) standing up to the Soviets, which implied rebuilding and modernizing the armed forces, and (2) checking the perceived Soviet gains in the Third World. The administration felt that the world was no longer convinced that the United States had the will to respond to military challenges and that this perception had led to increased challenges to U.S. interests by the Soviets and others. The

Reagan administration came into office prepared to flex its military muscle. It was, however, noticeably more strident toward small, peripheral countries over which it knew that it had a definite advantage. This is how one military analyst saw the situation that time: "When Alexander Haig was Secretary of State, the decision to respond to Soviet provocation had been focused on El Salvador. When the situation proved to be increasingly complex, the Reagan administration determined that Grenada was the place to 'stand tall,' to re-establish U.S. military credibility."[1]

The problem with this approach was that the policymakers were taking a rather narrow and simplistic view of events in these countries. Certainly there was a strong left-wing, even Communist, element in all of the revolutionary movements, but it was the local political and economic conditions that bred these indigenous revolutionary situations. In some cases it was the backing of past U.S. administrations that allowed corrupt, despotic politicians and military governments to continue to hang on. This was indeed the case in Grenada and Nicaragua. It was U.S. inattention to the economic decline in Latin America over several administrations that allowed the countries to search for a radical alternative. One British scholar saw the situation in this way: "Thus for a long time the Americans have been neglecting their Latin American neighbours owing to the strategic loneliness of the continent, and have been giving relatively more support to weak friends threatened by communism than more faithful and stable ones."[2] U.S. policy tends to put an emphasis on areas of high and visible Communist activity. Little wonder, then, that many brutal dictators contend that political agitation is Communist inspired and justify new rounds of repression as attempts to get rid of Communists, and in doing so feel assured of retaining U.S. support. U.S. policymakers have a blind spot toward anything labelled Communist.

But whatever the problems with its approach, the administration needed to show its resolve, as many writers observed. Reagan administration policy was to use opposition of a perceived Communist threat in a Third World country to restore American self-confidence and demonstrate to others that the U.S. military threat was still potent as the administration pursued its foreign policy objectives. It was this understanding that caused the governments of Grenada to build and strengthen their own armed forces.

Prior to coming into office, American political conservatives had

begun to point to Grenada as one more country that had been "lost."
Grenada and Cuba were the only countries in the Western Hemisphere
to vote against the UN resolution in 1980 that called upon the Soviets
to withdraw from Afghanistan. This vote was held up as clear evidence
that those governments had fallen into the Soviet orbit. Thereafter,
unofficial sources had the Soviets building a secret submarine base on
Grenada.[3] These reports were picked up and given wide publicity in
the United States and abroad.

It was not until nearly three years later, in 1983, that the *Washington
Post*, after sending a reporter on a visit, was able to report that the story
was totally without foundation. Reagan administration policy toward
Grenada had been conducted from the beginning on the basis of a lie.
Not long after the story of the secret submarine base was floated, a
report was circulated about the secret construction of a military airbase
by the Soviets and Cubans, equally true. These were the firm foundations
upon which the Reagan administration decision makers began their terms
in government.

Once Grenada has been identified as a problem nation with which
the administration was going to have to deal, each department set about
making its own plans for such an eventuality. As would be expected,
this stage of the administration policy planning meant that the relevant
departments would each prepare their own groundwork for any operation
that might have to be undertaken.

The State Department, in charge of the day-to-day execution of U.S.
foreign policy, was already disengaged from Grenada when the Reagan
administration took over. The Carter administration had instructed the
U.S. ambassador not to visit the island nation in protest against its anti-
American statements. This policy was continued by the incoming Reagan administration. Repeated efforts by Maurice Bishop himself to get
a U.S. ambassador to visit the island went unanswered by the State
Department. This decision might well have deprived the administration
of a firsthand view of what was going on inside Grenada; instead the
United States opted for no contact.

This policy seemed odd and inconsistent to many Caribbean scholars
and journalists when they saw the same administration adhering to a
policy of "constructive engagement" with the government of South
Africa. Knowing the real situation in Grenada—that there was no secret
submarine base and that the airport being constructed was neither secret
nor military—many Caribbean political groups construed the attacks by

Washington on Grenada as racist. As a result, they were willing to give Bishop the benefit of the doubt or were mute in their criticism, and were instead critical of Reagan administration policy. This criticism some U.S. journalists saw as anti-American. To the Caribbean political activists it was a question of principle, humanity, and fairness; to the administration it was a question of politics. Reagan administration policy was preoccupied with the Soviet challenge, and South Africa was fiercely anticommunist. That the U.S. policy toward Grenada could be based on such fantasy, while its policy toward South Africa showed such understanding, left Caribbean academics and political activists perplexed and frustrated. When U.S. journalists failed to see this, they were accused by these Caribbeans of being supportive of administration policy.

Having consistently ignored Grenada's request for a U.S. ambassador to be assigned to the island, the U.S. State Department then sought to convince its main allies in the EEC to follow suit. But the EEC countries listened to Grenada's appeal for aid and, despite U.S. pressure, contributed to the financing of the construction of the airport. Theirs was an economic decision, to aid a project that they were convinced would benefit the people of Grenada. Politically they remained tight-lipped about Grenada-U.S. differences. Britain at first tended to support the negative U.S. position, then adopted the EEC position after realizing that a British firm had been awarded the contract for one aspect of the airport construction.

To increase the pressure on Grenada, which seemed to be doing well in soliciting aid abroad, the State Department put Grenada on its list of nations that tourists should bypass. This policy was meant to sever a main artery of Grenada's financial support, and this it did. Grenada countered by inviting at its own expense a group of travel writers to see conditions for themselves and so dispel the fear that was generated by the administration. But the damage was already done, as travel writers then had to give political explanations to calm those fears before commenting on the tourist infrastructure and advantages.

Despite the lack of an ambassador or diplomatic staff on Grenada, the State Department remained active from afar in opposing the government of Grenada and in monitoring events there. U.S. pressure had succeeded in sapping the energy of the NJM government as it fought to counter U.S. disinformation, loss of tourism, and isolation. The constant threat of invasion had also caused the government to become preoccupied with internal security, which caused even greater resentment among the people.

Having failed to persuade Washington to establish diplomatic relations over a number of years, and faced with increased pressure from within his own party to mollify Washington or support an all-out Stalinist policy, Bishop flew to Washington in a desperate attempt to mend fences in June 1983. The meeting he sought with President Reagan was rejected out of hand. It was suggested instead that he see a low-level diplomat, which Bishop rejected as inappropriate. It was only then that a compromise was reached: Bishop met and talked with Lawrence Eagleburger and Kenneth Dam of the State Department and William Clark, head of the National Security Council.

The administration's reluctance to see Bishop after years of pressure suggests either that it was caught up in bureaucratic inertia that prevented it from undertaking a change in policy, or that it was content to see him as a Communist enemy because it suited its domestic political posture to do so. Or it could well be that it was reluctant to admit that it had made a mistake and was fearful of retracting its position. No one thought or proposed that Bishop might be worth cultivating. Indeed, cultivating a leader who originally opposes or angers U.S. policymakers has not been high on the lists of diplomatic tasks for policymakers of either party.

Bishop's impetuous visit to Washington was the latest in a long list of efforts by Third World leaders beginning with Mao Tse-tung who had asked either to go to Washington or to discuss relations at a high level and had been politely refused or grudgingly accommodated. This has prompted some to wonder whether an underlying current in the mind of policymakers is not the constant fear of seeming to be "soft" on communism. This notion has been suspected as the reason for several U.S. adventures in the recent past. One group of scholars analyzing the decision to go into Korea wondered aloud: "Suppose, for example, that the real yet unexpressed reason for a strong, positive response to the North Korean invasion was the prevailing domestic political climate, one component of which was the oft-repeated charge that the administration was 'soft' on communism and that officials had 'sold out' in China."[4] Thus the failure to make a diplomatic effort to reach an accommodation with Grenada seems to have met a traditional response. Perhaps this is the reason why, for most of this century, the United States has not had diplomatic relations with one country or another.

The next agency that had an input into the pre-decision-making stage of the administration policy was the CIA. Its function was to collect and analyze all relevant information about Grenada and to plan all clandestine operations. We can assume that plans were drawn up for the possible destabilization of Grenada. Bishop indeed mentioned that he had proof of such a plan. Secret as such a plan would be, one can only surmise that he was able to get wind of it because the CIA itself leaked the news to keep up the pressure on Bishop and his colleagues. On several occasions Bishop blamed the CIA for acts of sabotage that occurred in Grenada. These accusations cannot be totally discounted; however, it is known that some founding members of his NJM party may well have engaged in some of these acts. It is suspected too that Bishop himself knew this, but blamed the CIA as a means of keeping his own domestic supporters alert.

For a big power the military is a very important component of its foreign policy apparatus. For most countries the military is an instrument of defense. But for more powerful nations it is a means of projecting power beyond its shores: its role is both offensive and defensive. "The credibility of a state's military forces (based on its record) is an important factor in its ability to gain its foreign policy objectives without the use of force. The threat of force is often sufficient to gain policy objectives."[5] But the military threat is only effective when combined with specific political goals and objectives; by itself it is most often ruthless.

In preparing its plan for action in Grenada, the U.S. military was painfully aware that it had lost some of its credibility as a military threat. Since World War II the U.S. military had suffered a series of small reverses and stalemates in its overseas adventures. Those that were won were noticeable for their poor planning and execution.

The Reagan administration had come into office convinced that the military had been unnecessarily maligned in the past, and that it shortcomings were due to inadequate financing and especially to excessive political supervision. The administration was determined to rid the body politic (and the military) of what was referred to as the "Vietnam syndrome." Based on its experience in Vietnam, the United States, including its political and military leadership, had become cautious about using the military as a substitute for clear political objectives, especially if there was not strong popular support for such action. It was a lesson that had been learned the hard way by both Republicans and Democrats, but obviously not by everyone. The extreme Right was always convinced that lack of financing, lack of resolve, and lack of management were the causes of America's failure. For them the application of an enormous quantity of firepower would break the will of any enemy to resist. It was a philosophy that many recognized did not work in Vietnam.

But these arguments stray from the central point: the force of nationalism gives people a fierce determination to fight for independence and freedom from domination in a way that differs radically from the motivation of a soldier fighting on governmental orders. The leaders of these nationalistic groups are also better educated, more skilled, and more determined than ever before. It is a lesson that every European colonial power learned the hard way: the Dutch in Indonesia, the British in India and Kenya, the French in Vietnam and Algeria, the Belgians in the Congo, and the Portuguese in Angola and Mozambique. None of these recognized the legitimate aspirations of those they dominated, though, until it was forcefully brought home to them. In some cases these wars have lasted for generations and could conceivably continue indefinitely. But the nationalistic groups all have shown a determination to win, if now now, in the future. It is the philosophy of the future that sustains them and makes such groups a nightmare for gunboat diplomacy. Military adventures, by their nature, must be reasonably short and must show clear and quick results. Miscalculations can have disastrous consequences for the government and the body politic, as the Suez crisis did in Britain, the Algerian revolution did in France, and the Vietnam War did in the United States. This does not mean that military adventures are bad, just that they are tricky. They have become an extremely high-risk policy to pursue.

But the precedents of the old order die hard, since some continue to believe that gunboat diplomacy will impress the natives. In today's atmosphere of heightened political awareness, however, a better-educated nationalistic population that has learned from the failed uprisings of the past is more likely to challenge the status quo than fear it. Except in isolated instances, foreign adventures cannot be really successful. Grenada was just such a case; it offered ideal circumstances for an invasion. Small, isolated, inhabited by a disgruntled population—it was a military planner's dream.

The U.S. military would have been remiss in its duties had it not prepared scenarios for a possible Grenada operation. In August 1981 U.S. and NATO forces, including British and Dutch vessels, took part in operation "Ocean Venture 81." These military maneuvers took place in the Atlantic and the Caribbean. A mock invasion was staged to rescue Americans held hostage on the island of "Amber" (Vieques, off Puerto Rico). Needless to say, the NJM government in Grenada was alarmed at the closeness of the exercises and the not-so-subtle attempt to intimidate it. Coming as early as the exercises did in the life of the Reagan administration, they made the government take the threat of invasion very seriously. It redoubled its efforts to raise and equip an army and prepare a civil defense for its island nation. In so doing it became even more heavily involved with the Soviets and other Eastern bloc states, for it was to them that the Grenada government had to turn for material after being rejected by Britain and other EEC states. These was the only publicized exercises held that seemed to be specifically directed at Grenada. However, the exercises held by the U.S. military in Central America, though a little more remote, served the same purpose.

Another government agency that monitored events in Grenada was the National Security Council. The National Security Council was established in 1947 "to advise the President with respect to the integration of domestic, foreign and military policies relating to the national security as to enable the military services and other departments agencies of the government to cooperate more effectively in matters involving national security."[6] Under President Reagan the NSC reflected the President's political preference in its composition, and despite its stormy history, it kept a close eye on Grenada.

The opinion of the NSC was shaped by the views of the ultraconservative Heritage Foundation and by a number of former intelligence and military officers who had become consultants in the Washington area. In fact, the Reagan administration seemed to be heavily influenced by ex-intelligence persons, military men, and scholars who specialized in these areas, giving the impression of an overreliance on the military option. So strong a staff of like mind seemed to give little consideration to options for the president but much to a view of how to proceed. According to some sources, this was the way President Reagan liked his staff to operate.

The original actions of the different departments in the U.S. government that were responsible for some aspect of the overall Grenada policy did not prepare them for final decisions that had to be taken. Implementing policy is very different from dealing with a crisis. In a crisis the quick change of events demands information and a rethinking of the strategy that had initially looked so good. Decision making in a crisis involves a review of pre-decision-making strategy and information as well as of the new information coming in.

The sudden knowledge that Maurice Bishop, the prime minister of Grenada, had been put under house arrest came as a complete surprise to Washington policymakers: they had operated under the assumption that he was totally in charge. Indeed, Washington often assumes that nondemocratic governments are monolithic in their composition, making it pointless even to try to reason with them. Suddenly, though, Reagan administration officials realized that there was a group within Bishop's NJM party that was even more doctrinaire than he.

The immediate concern was for the U.S. citizens on the island, in particular the medical students. Everyone was anxious that there should not be a repeat of the experience of the Carter administration, with hostages taken and the U.S. publicly held helpless by a group of fanatics. It appears that the military option was the first to be explored. While the cabinet of the island of Barbados was discussing the problem and giving serious thought to some type of attempt to rescue Bishop, word came that the United States was thinking along the same lines. This low-level inquiry, which was revealed by Prime Minister Adams, could have been a personal message or perhaps a fishing expedition by some agency hoping to make a policy proposal in Washington. This interest on the part of any U.S. agency is curious in view of the administration's stormy relationship with Bishop. It could have been a belated attempt to correct U.S. misperception of the Grenada political situation from the beginning. If the rescue proposal was genuine, it would have been a spectacular undertaking, but to what end? It is doubtful whether a U.S.-rescued Bishop would have had the same confidence and support to govern effectively, even with U.S. and Caribbean help.

Formal planning by the United States for some type of involvement in the Grenada crisis began on October 17, 1983. Prior to that date, a secret gathering had been taking place regularly at the State Department. The Restricted Interagency Group was formed in 1981 by then Assistant Secretary of State for Inter-American Affairs Thomas O. Enders to formulate policy and monitor events in problem countries. At its inception the group, chaired by Enders, also included Duane Clarridge of the CIA an expert on covert operations; Vice Admiral Arthur S. Morean, Jr., a representative of the Joint Chiefs of Staff; and Nestor Sanchez, a representative of the office of the secretary of defense. At the time of the Grenada invasion, Langhorne A. Motley was assistant secretary of state for inter-American affairs, and Colonel Oliver North of the NSC had become a member of the group.[7] By this time the role of the group had changed. Rather than formulating policy, the group had become a catalyst and initiator of ideas for the destabilization or disruption of those governments that resist U.S. policy. After hatching these ideas, the members then tried to sell them to their departments. Because the White House (through the NSC) was represented, each member could claim that the idea had the backing of the other departments and the highest authority.

That this group was concerned primarily with the military option of dealing with other countries was supported by the mood that emanated from the administration itself. But it also stemmed from a deep fear by the administration of being caught flat-footed in a situation akin to Jimmy Carter's experience in Iran. At the meeting of October 17 the discussion centered on the fate of the U.S. citizens living on Grenada and especially on the possibility of them being taken hostage. The Defense Department favored an Entebbe-style rescue: highly trained troops sent in to pluck the hostages from their captors in a surprise attack, followed by a quick withdrawal to safety. The Defense Department officials were particularly wary of anything more than a short, swift operation since it was already also engaged in a trying peace-keeping operation in Lebanon. They were also unwilling to engage in further planning unless they were sure that such a military option was being considered at a higher level.

The same group met again on October 19 to discuss the unexpected development of Bishop's death. The positions taken were essentially the same as in the first meeting. The main concern was for the safety of U.S. citizens and the desirability of averting a long hostage crisis. That evening Assistant Secretary of State Langhorne Motley was called to brief Secretary Shultz on the Grenada situation and to give him a sense of the feeling of the different department representatives of the interagency group.

By October 20, 1983, Prime Minister Adams of Barbados and other

OECS head of government had already decided individually that they wanted some sort of military action against Grenada—an invasion. Exploratory talks with the British, Canadian, and U.S. ambassadors were held. These informal talks prompted the State Department in Washington to send its own personal point man, Charles Gillespie, to Barbados. This move showed tremendous foresight. Having been caught short by not foreseeing a split in Maurice Bishop's party, much less his subsequent execution, the department determined to maintain close contact with the neighboring governments. It wanted to have not only reliable feedback but also a voice. It seems clear from the events that followed that U.S. policymakers were already aware of the gravity of the request for assistance and the criticism they were likely to face if they obliged—hence the frantic footwork, intended to give an air of legality to their actions.

The drastic changes that had occurred in Grenada and the reaction of the neighboring Caribbean governments raised the level of concern and the possibility of involvement of Washington. Rather than thinking in a reactive manner about what should be done to forestall a hostage crisis or protect U.S. citizens should the situation in Grenada worsen, the United States was instead being asked to consider invasion—invasion as a partner, by invitation. That was new, something different. This curious situation aroused the interest of everyone. The task force steaming to the Middle East to keep the peace in Beirut was diverted to the Caribbean as a precaution in case it was needed and was now better positioned for action, given that an invitation was likely to be forthcoming to invade Grenada.

That Friday evening, October 21, the president left Washington, D.C., for a weekend of rest and recreation of golf in Augusta, Georgia. Also on that very evening the OECS heads of government held a meeting in Barbados and agreed to ask the United States to intervene. Their invitation was delivered to the U.S. ambassador, Milan Bish, and to Anthony Gillespie in Barbados later that evening. Secretary of State Shultz, travelling with the president, was awakened at 2:45 A.M. Saturday with the news.

The Caribbean countries urged that Washington move quickly for fear that the news would leak out and give the Cubans and Grenadians time to prepare their defenses. Sunday, October 23, they said, would be the best day to strike.[8] Secretary Shultz discussed the now-confirmed developments with newly appointed National Security Adviser Robert

McFarlane. Vice President Bush, the administration's crisis manager, convened a meeting of the NSC on October 22. It was a time for decisions. The State Department's view was argued by Lawrence Eagleburger. He raised the specter of an Iran hostage–type affair if the United States did nothing. He argued further that to do nothing would cause the United States to lose face in the Caribbean and in Central America at a time when toughness was called for, especially given the challenges to Washington from left-wing governments in the area. Pentagon officials cautioned against a hurried operation in Grenada. They reasoned that the earliest such an operation could be readied was Wednesday, October 26, or maybe the twenty-fifth if absolutely required. The president himself participated in this meeting by phone from Georgia, thus reassuring the NSC members of the extreme consideration their views were getting.

The next day, at 2:27 A.M., President Reagan was awakened in Augusta, Georgia, by National Security Adviser Robert McFarlane with the news that the marine Corps headquarters in Beirut had been bombed and that forty-six marines were known to be dead, with many more probably dead in the rubble. The administration's Middle East policy was dealt a stunning setback, and this event raised the stakes of any decision that was to be made about Grenada. The administration's Middle East policy had already been under sharp criticism as Lebanese snipers had continued their attacks on the marines and as casualties had been sustained.

The president and his entourage returned to Washington early on Sunday morning. A meeting of the National Security Council was convened and ran throughout the day. By late afternoon the president agreed to authorize a full-scale invasion in conjunction with forces from the OECS nations. One unconfirmed source maintains that President Reagan wavered about making a final decision and only did so when Eugenia Charles, the prime minister of Dominica, was brought to the White House by friends from the American Enterprise Institute and put her case directly to him. Though unconfirmed, the story seems plausible and shows how serious the Caribbean governments of the OECS group were in their call for an invasion. But it also shows the interest and influence of outside groups on policy and decisions.

The NSC would have had a number of concerns before making up its mind as to whether to support the call for an invasion. The primary concern most likely was the anticipated reaction of world opinion and in particular Latin American opinion to yet another U.S. invasion. Because the United States has been involved in invasions of Latin American countries thirty-three times in the last century, the two continents have become rather wary of each other in this regard. But the other overriding consideration was the re-election of the president. Because he had been elected on the basis that he would be tough with challenges to U.S. power in the Third World, the debacle in Beirut looked like a tremendous failure. A bold move was required to restore the president's credibility, especially as new elections approached. That the decision to go for an invasion was made was due to good staff work by the State Department and the NSC and the luck of having a number of relatively conservative Caribbean governments in office at that time who favored an encouraged invasion.

It is ironic that the invasion was seen eventually as such a success for the Reagan administration. When he assumed office, his policy was to bring the government of Grenada to its senses and to pressure it to abandon its close relationships with Cuba and the Soviet Union. Rather than doing so, Grenada moved closer to those countries. Invasion demonstrated the failure of U.S. policy to achieve the desired results after three years of U.S. pressure and isolation. That the administration's Grenada policy was a failure was overshadowed by the excitement of the invasion and what its success meant for the American body politic: military success, at last, and an apparent end to the "Vietnam syndrome." But the confusion of military success with policy success fools no one but U.S. policymakers themselves, and has led to continued misinterpretations of foreign policy successes. As a result, mistakes are frequently repeated.

To the Commonwealth Caribbean nations the results of U.S. policy decisions seemed different from what was intended. The Caribbean governments were fearful of the United States and any premature action it might take. The first reaction of the Caribbean governments was to try to pressure the Grenadian government to conform to the preferences of the Caribbean people and other governments of the region for some type of parliamentary government. Their most immediate concern was to see the NJM hold elections and free its political prisoners. Contrary to the policy of the Caribbean governments, the main thrust of U.S. policy was to see Grenada sever its relationships with Cuba and the Soviets. While many Caribbean governments were finding great difficulty in dealing with their mounting deficits and falling aid, Grenada seemed to be faring much better. U.S. talk about a submarine base and a military airport was known to be false. The Caribbean governments knew that the airport under construction was an economic project with which Grenada had wrestled for some time; they themselves had had difficulty financing similar projects. The accusations by the United States were seen as an attempt to set up Grenada for a possible military move to satisfy its own preoccupation with Communist influence in the hemisphere and the Third World.

When President Reagan, on holiday in the Caribbean, pressed those leaders with whom he conferred to isolate Grenada, their response was evasive. They pressed him instead for an increase in aid and a greater share in the U.S. Caribbean Basin Initiative. Earlier, when the United States had tried to exclude Grenada from receiving U.S. aid disbursed through the Caribbean Development Bank, these countries had objected. Many activists, opposition parties, academics, and journalists, however, were offended at the mildness of the objections, which to them indicated undue respect for the U.S. position. They pointed out regularly that the United States, while pressing others to isolate Grenada, treated South Africa differently under the policy of "constructive engagement." They asserted that U.S. policy was hypocritical and saw the tone of U.S. criticism as sanctimonious and offensive. Their criticism of U.S. policy was often couched in terms of the American legacy of slavery and racial discrimination and the inability of U.S. policymakers and diplomats to rise above their cultural roots.

While there may be a considerable element of truth in these accusations, most U.S. policymakers tend to fall into the mental trap of thinking that because Third world leaders come from backward societies, they are backward also. They seem to forget that though many of these leaders might come from relatively primitive societies, they are societies that are by and large primitive but not provincial. These were criticisms that all of the Caribbean governments had to take seriously. But governments are also concerned with staying in power, and critics and activists are interested in pointing out inconsistencies in the status quo with the hope of gaining office or changing policy.

The critics of the Caribbean governments which only gave mild support to Grenada were particularly effective, since two decades earlier other peoples of the Caribbean had been in the similar position of seeking to pull away from an oppressive and stagnant colonial power. The governments, however, while uneasy, knew that while the general population might be sympathetic with the South Africa problem, they saw it as extraneous to the severe economic problems they were facing in their everyday lives. While critical of their own governments' succumbing to the U.S. opposition groups and political activists, they were not quick to praise the government of Grenada either, as the relatively attractive image of an energetic idealistic Grenada revolution deteriorated over the years into that of a repressive regime.

On the other hand, the U.S. administration's foreign policy decisions were generally viewed somewhat differently. The president's views and those of his administration were given prominence in the press and media, but when the press's own investigation discovered facts to the contrary, these were not given the same prominence. Therefore a view persisted that Grenada had become closely allied to Cuba and the Soviets, and more dangerously, that the Cubans were constructing an airport for military use on the island. Grenada, as the Reagan administration presented it to the people of the United States, was a threat to the United States and to the hemisphere. Faced with a Nicaragua that leaned toward Cuba and the Soviets in Central America, and with other guerrilla groups active in that area, the administration felt that it had to take a firm stand against these challenges to U.S. hegemony. A serious, perhaps military, response was needed to satisfy the widely held view (planted by the Reagan administration) that the Communists were on the march in the hemisphere, and to fulfill its election promise that it would do something about it. This was the reason why the Restricted Interagency Group, formed by the State Department, evolved so easily from a policy formulation and assessment group into one of military planning and covert operations. A request for an invasion of Grenada fitted neatly into the administration's desires and plans for both ideological and political reasons. Military victory begets patriotic fervor and obscures a failure of policy; the trouble is that too often in the recent past military success has been confused with policy success.

As far as the domestic U.S. political reaction was concerned, the invasion was a success, even if poorly executed. It showed the administration as being "tough on communism" and willing to roll back Communist gains in a Third World country. It spelled an end to the Vietnam syndrome, as the administration saw it, and it avoided a possible hostage crisis. Even though only some elements of these points were true, the majority of the population does not pay strict attention to the details of operations; their concerns tend to be more general. The negatives were a small minority, as few within the Congress, academia, the media, or among political activists questioned the government's action.

But once the invasion was complete, the administration sought to make more of its victory than was there, for both political and policy reasons. The military victory and the sight of the returning American students kissing U.S. soil as they stepped off the military aircraft that brought them home gave the administration great confidence. It engendered increased political support and patriotic fervor. This heightened approval of the president's handling of a foreign crisis quickly obscured the Beirut bombing of a few days before and caused an elated President Reagan to announce to the nation that America was "standing tall" again. But the simple announcement of a politician, or his will, does not make it so. While the president can influence the people of the United States, who are predisposed to believe in their own success, he does not have the same influence with people outside the United States. Outsiders deal with the facts as they see them, with their own biases and preconceptions.

The attempts to overstate the Grenada victory and give it a wider meaning than it actually had do not help United States policy for the future. They make the Reagan administration look good in its effort to have the media and constituents draw conclusions favorable to itself. The result is that true believers are misled, and the policy debate continues on faulty premises.

NOTES

1. Richard A. Gabriel, *Military Incompetence: Why the American Military Doesn't Win* (New York: Hill and Wang, 1985), p. 150.

2. Joseph Frankel, *The Making of Foreign Policy: Analysis of Decision-Making* (New York: Oxford University Press, 1971), p. 178.

3. Hugh O'Shaughnessy, *Grenada: An Eyewitness Account of the U.S. Invasion and the Caribbean History That Provoked It* (New York: Dodd, Mead and Company, 1984), p. 194.

4. Richard C. Snyder, H. W. Bruck, and Burton Sapin, eds. *Foreign Policy Decisionmaking: An Approach to the Study of International Politics* (New York: The Free Press, 1962), p. 21.

5. Gabriel, *Military Incompetence*, p. 3.

6. At the time of the Grenada invasion, the NSC proper was composed of

the president (Ronald Reagan), the vice president (George Bush), the secretary of state (George Shultz), the secretary of defense (Caspar Weinberger), the chairman of the Joint Chiefs of Staff (General John Vessey), and the CIA director (William Casey). These officials were served by a staff of people directed by the national security adviser, Robert McFarlane.

7. Keith Schneider North, "Record: A Wide Role in a Host of Sensitive Projects," *New York Times*, January 3, 1987.

8. O'Shaughnessy, *Grenada*, p. 16.

9

Interim Government and Post-Invasion Politics

Once the invasion was complete, the leaders of the People's Revolutionary Government were arrested by the U.S. forces, and after questioning, eighteen were handed over to the local authorities. They were then charged with the deaths of Maurice Bishop and his colleagues. The only person left with any authority was Governor General Sir Paul Scoon, Grenada's representative of Queen Elizabeth II. The queen resided in London and Sir Paul in Grenada; both found themselves in a quandary before the dust finally settled. She was queen of Jamaica, Barbados, St. Kitts-Nevis, St. Lucia, and St. Vincent, all of whose governments supported the invasion. But she was also the head of the Commonwealth that included Belize, Guyana, and Trinidad and Tobago, whose governments opposed the invasion. Whose position was she supposed to represent?

These may be fine points of protocol, but what really matters is that in fact the institution worked and did so remarkably well. Having been appointed by Gairy and ignored by the NJM, Scoon was the one nonpartisan figure to whom people could look when the crisis left the island without political leadership. As soon as the invasion had ended, the governor general moved to take charge. He swung into action with such zest and savvy that many people were taken by surprise.

Having reestablished contact with Buckingham Palace and the Commonwealth Office in London, both of which were concerned for his safety, he began working closely with newly appointed U.S. Ambassador Designate Charles Gillespie. On October 31, in his first proclamation, he announced that he was forming an advisory council or interim government to help him administer the affairs of the country until elections could be held. While Gillespie favored the idea of an interim government, he did not altogether like its composition. In this area Sir Paul had had the advice of the Commonwealth Secretariat in London, and in particular the advice of Secretary General Shridath Ramphal, the former foreign minister of Guyana, who was well known to him. Ramphal impressed on Sir Paul the need to move quickly on the formation of an interim government that would take care of the day-to-day administration, the need for early elections, and, most of all, the need to press for the quick withdrawal of U.S. forces from the island. It was Ramphal's concern that the continued presence of U.S. troops on the island of Grenada could cause a serious split among the commonwealth Caribbean nations.

The chairmanship of the advisory council was offered to a Grenadian international civil servant, Alister McIntyre, deputy secretary general of the UN Conference on Trade and Development. Prior to that, he had had a fine career as an economist at the University of the West Indies and had been closely associated with Caricom and other regional organizations. Everyone, including those opposed to the invasion, cheered Scoon's selection. Another appointee to the advisory council was Patrick Emmanuel, a university lecturer who had been a vocal supporter of Bishop's strategy and was known for his controversial views in the region. In the end, McIntyre could not take the post for health and other reasons, and it was given to another civil servant, Nicholas Bratwaite, who worked within the region.

The original announcement of the composition of the advisory council helped dispel much of the fear of the Caribbean people that Grenada would become just another American puppet. The Reagan administration was not altogether pleased with the appointments, but was even less pleased with Scoon's announcement that elections would be held within a year. At the very least, the administration felt that a period of two years was necessary to give the parties time to regroup. Although the administration and Ambassador Gillespie differed with Sir Paul on his political choices, these differences actually boosted his image and showed him to be a skilled political maneuverer. Ironically, the economic project that everyone, including the new government, wanted to see completed was the new airport at Point Salines. Even more bizarre was the fact that the Reagan administration, which was so opposed to its construction on strategic grounds, was now prepared to finance its completion. A $43 million aid package was negotiated with the United States for 1984 in addition to the substantial amounts of emergency aid granted immediately after the invasion. One project that received particular attention was the special service unit within the police force. With the training of local law enforcement forces completed, the last of the substantially diminished U.S. forces left in June 1985.

The U.S. forces had behaved themselves well once the fighting had ended. They allowed the Caribbean troops and police to join with them in restoring order and in maintaining security. They were friendly, helpful, and courteous to the Grenadians, even as they made spot checks of cars or conducted searches. Most of all, they tried to return the domestic situation to normal by removing military hardware from sight and from inconvenient areas as soon as possible. The speed with which they set up offices to receive claims for damage caused to property by the invading U.S. forces and their political tack of flying the Grenada flag along with their own did much to endear them to Grenadians.[1]

Political jockeying among hopeful parties began almost as soon as word of the invasion became known. Sir Eric Gairy, resident in the United States, let it be known through several interviews that he still considered himself to be the rightfully elected leader of Grenada and intended to return to reclaim his position. The main Caribbean leaders who supported the invasion agreed to his return, but not as president. His property, which had been seized by the NJM government, would be returned to him in return for his promise not to run for political office again. The agreement did not, however, preclude a reconstituted Gairy party (GULP) from political activity under a new head, a small detail that worried some people who envisaged a clever Gairy using a political stand-in for a while only to retake the leadership later. This was another bold and daring move by the Caribbean governments most involved in the domestic affairs of Grenada, and shows both the extent to which those governments were independent of Washington and their desire to monitor post-revolutionary developments in Grenada.

Another veteran politician, Herbert Blaize, was quick to announce that he had also not retired from politics and would reactivate his party. During the time that the NJM was in power, Blaize had been on Grenada's sister island of Carriacou, his stronghold, away from the center of activity, and had survived. But his survival itself is a commentary on his political stature, for the NJM never considered him or his supporters a group passionate enough to mount a serious challenge to them.

The other political parties functioning abroad in various stages of growth began to return to Grenada. The Grenada Democratic Movement (GDM), headed by university lecturer Francis Alexis, returned from its bases in Barbados and the United States. A new party, the National Democratic Party (NDP), was established by George Brizen in February 1984. Winston Whyte established the Christian Democratic Labour Party (CDLP). The NJM, never the mass political party it had always wanted to be, was reformed under two of Bishop's ex-ministers, George Louison and Kendrick Radix, as the Maurice Bishop Patriotic Movement (MBPM).

Within a few weeks a number of the parties decided to merge. The veteran Herbert Blaize and his GNP decided to merge with the GDM and the NDP under the new name the Team of National Togetherness. Elections were set for December 5, 1984. As the elections approached, the Team of National Togetherness broke up over Herbert Blaize's attempt to make his faction dominant and his insistence on a personal veto over all election candidates the party fielded. But even as they broke up, each of the parties was seeking an alliance with another. Their main fear was that alone and untested they were no match for the once-popular and now-reformed Grenada United Labour Party (GULP), once headed by Gairy. However, none of the mergers lasted for very long, although the main leaders always kept talking about the possibility. Eventually, the GNP of Herbert Blaize and the GDM headed by Francis Alexis merged to form the Team of National Unity.

With elections fast approaching, those of Grenada's neighbors who had sanctioned and participated in the invasion were becoming restless with the squabbling between the parties. In August a number of leaders—Adams (Barbados), Mitchell (St. Vincent), and Compton (St. Lucia)—called the protagonists to a meeting on Union Island, an outer island that forms part of St. Vincent. At that meeting a merger was agreed to, with the veteran Herbert Blaize as the leader of a group named the New National Party (NNP). In the weeks preceding the Union Island meeting, the U.S. representatives had also become disheartened by the squabbling among the parties and had made it known that U.S. aid would probably cease should the GULP gain a victory in the forthcoming elections. These fears prompted Grenada's neighbors to once again exert their personal influence in Grenada's internal affairs. After the formation of the NNP, the Reagan administration arranged for a number of private companies and organizations to make donations to its campaign. On the eve of the election the tiny CDLP, headed by Winston Whyte, dropped out of the NNP. When the elections were held on December 5, 1984, the NNP won fifteen seats and the formerly Gairy-led GULP won one seat. It was a sweeping victory for the new party. But even though it won only one seat, the GULP showed that it was still a potent force in the political life of the country, gaining 36 percent of the vote. The former NJM, now the Maurice Bishop Patriotic Movement (MBPM), did not win a single seat.

Soon after the election, the NNP government under Prime Minister Herbert Blaize began to show signs of disunity. Cabinet members have continued to coalesce around the leader of the party from which they came originally. This situation is exacerbated by the frequent absence of the prime minister on government business overseas, by his reluctance to discuss and debate policy, and by the general arbitrary nature of his leadership. Prime Minister Blaize, a man in poor health and advanced in age, probably realizes that this may well be the last government with which he will be associated and is determined to do things as he sees fit. Not many people, however, have ever thought of him as an imaginative leader, and this is reflected in the polls. There is every possibility that his actions will precipitate the disintegration of the NNP, with each faction returning to its former party. At that point, the leadership of each party can claim to have had some experience in government.

NOTE

1. Hugh O'Shaughnessy, *Grenada: An Eyewitness Account of the U.S. Invasion and the Caribbean History That Provoked It* (New York: Dodd, Mead and Company, 1984), p. 180.

10

Regional Intervention in the Caribbean

The law regarding intervention in one state by another is written in the Charter of the United Nations and is quite clear. It permits the use of force only in the case of self-defense or against "armed attack." It also sanctions such action when properly authorized by the United Nations. The other agreement to which the United States and other member countries within this hemisphere adhere is the Charter of the Organization of American States. It too is clear on the subject of intervention: "The territory of a State is inviolable; it may not be the object, even temporarily, of military occupation or of other measures of force taken by another State, directly or indirectly, on any grounds whatever." The only exception to this provision is action taken "in accordance with existing treaties," that being the United Nations Charter.

While all nations are concerned with general international order, the evolution of subregional and regional variations of that order has been evident for some time. In the UN itself blocs have developed, such as the Afro-Asian bloc, the Latin American bloc, and the EEC group. While some groups are political in nature, a member often joins an economic or military alliance without the others of its political group. A typical example is Japan, which finds itself part of "the affluent alliance" when economics is discussed, part of the Asian group when politics is discussed, and not part of NATO. In the same vein the English-speaking Caribbean countries, by custom and by preference, have carved a niche for themselves within the Caribbean area, even though they also recognize and belong to the larger hemispheric grouping. As a result, a pattern of culture, economics, and politics has developed in the area that has allowed the group to act as a loose federation. Grenada is a long-standing member of this subregional group.

The island was made part of the Windward Islands Administration under the British Crown in 1833 and was administered as a part of this group until 1958, when the administration was dissolved. In 1958 the Federation of the West Indies was created, which included many of the larger islands in the area—Barbados, Trinidad and Tobago, and Jamaica—as well as the smaller islands in the archipelago. Grenada was also a member of this group. Internal disagreements within the federation caused it to collapse in 1962. As a result, for the first time in 129 years Grenada was completely on its own and not in an administrative or political association with any of its neighbors. It was at this time that the Grenada National Party won election to office based largely on a platform pledged to seek unitary statehood with Trinidad and Tobago. This was planned because Trinidad and Tobago's natural resources could sustain the inclusion of Grenada, and more importantly, there were as many Grenadians on Trinidad and Tobago as in Grenada itself. The unity talks broke down, however, and nothing came of the idea. In 1967 Grenada again joined its old associates to form the West Indies Associated States. This political grouping did for the ministates what was attempted and failed earlier in the larger grouping.

Despite political independence from Britain in 1974, Grenada continued to be a member of the Associated States. The political, economic, judicial, and cultural benefits that the group as a whole enjoyed made it more beneficial and cost-effective to remain a member of the group rather than go it alone. So throughout the last century and a half, Grenada has for one reason or another been closely linked with its immediate neighbors in an administrative and political sense. That these links continued voluntarily even after the island gained independence suggests the need the government and people felt to be in close contact with their neighbors and the compatibility they felt with them. While these associations may be seen by some as the necessary compromises a small island must make in finding the best practical way of preserving its independence, this is not likely. The evidence demonstrates that successive governments of Grenada trusted the judgments of the governments and people of the Caribbean area in some of their most trying times since independence. Apart from joining and participating in all of the regional political, economic, and cultural activities, successive administrations have at times invited their fellow citizens from the region to arbitrate some of their disputes.

Even in more serious cases when public order was threatened, help was sought from neighboring islands. The French Revolution of 1789 had very severe repercussions in the Caribbean and led to a black revolt and the establishment of the Republic of Haiti a few years later. A similar attempt was made in Grenada in 1795 when Julian Fedon, son of a French father and a slave mother, sought to lead a revolt against British colonial rule.[1] For over a year he fought the British and controlled most of the country with the exception of the capital, St. George's. The struggle, which claimed the life of British Governor Ninian Home and some fifty British citizens, only came to an end with the arrival of General Sir Ralph Abercromby, who with reinforcements from other British islands surrounded Fedon in an ambush and destroyed most of this group. Fedon himself escaped, and while official accounts list him as having died from exposure in the jungle or drowned in his attempts to escape to Trinidad, local legends speak of his survival and living on another island.

As recently as 1951 the people of other islands were again called upon to provide troops to restore order in Grenada when the British governor arrested Eric Gairy for organizing the island's first general strike and ordered him to be deported to the neighboring island of Carriacou. Violence and rioting broke out in Grenada, the governor requested further help as the violence continued, and the Royal Navy was sent in, together with a detachment of police from the neighboring islands of Trinidad, St. Lucia, Barbados, and Jamaica.[2] After eleven days of rioting and violence and the release of Gairy the situation was brought under control and order restored. The precedents of security assistance and cooperation were not lost on the people of Grenada or on the leaders of the other islands.

When the newly formed New Jewel Movement took up the case of Jerry Richardson, murdered by the police at Grenville in 1973, the government of Premier Eric Gairy, responding to the political and social pressure for an impartial inquiry, brought in a police officer from Trinidad and Tobago to conduct it. A few months later, when the political situation again got out of hand and the government found it necessary to appoint a commission to investigate the "Bloody Sunday" matter, it again reached outside the island. This time it appointed a three-man investigative commission: Sir Herbert Duffus and Archbishop Samuel

Carter of Jamaica, and Mr. Aubrey Fraser of Guyana. Even for the extremely delicate job of drafting a new constitution for Grenada, the Bishop government appointed a lawyer from neighboring Trinidad and Tobago.

The government of Grenada, as an independent and sovereign nation, could quite easily have found retired Grenadian judges, senior civil servants, and many others who would have given the commission the credibility it sought. It could have also appointed Grenadians working in prominent posts within the Caribbean region or in international organizations if it wanted to keep a nationalistic lid on the investigation. Instead it chose to go outside Grenada, a practice not common among sovereign nations, thus underlining the strong ties and confidence Grenada has in its regional neighbors.

But Grenada is not alone among the Commonwealth Caribbean island states in this regard. The practice of using, on a limited level, each other's personnel has been a tradition in the Caribbean for some time, especially in the areas of law and security. The sharing of a common university system, the University of the West Indies, with major resident campuses in Jamaica, Trinidad and Tobago, and Barbados has been a homogenizing factor that brings a number of future decision makers from the region together. When the common cricket team, the West Indies touring team, chosen from among the best cricketers of each territory, plays a foreign cricketing nation, the radio sets from one end of the Caribbean to the other are turned to the same commentary. From a number of standpoints the Commonwealth Caribbean community is much more closely integrated than its members' individual, independent status would suggest. A dramatic event that reflects this cooperation is the request from the prime minister of St. Vincent to the prime minister of Barbados for troops to assist in quelling civil disturbances on his island. The OECS countries, together with Barbados and Jamaica, presumed to make decisions for the sovereign nation of Grenada when it was deemed that there was a breakdown of law and order and that the military council could not consolidate power without the strong possibility of further bloodshed. Hence their decision to mount an invasion, arrest the problem, and restore order.

In simpler terms, a person who owns a piece of property is free to do inside its confines whatever he or she wishes. However if they were to start a large fire on their own property for their own personal enjoyment, they would alarm their neighbors, who would undoubtedly look on with concern. If the fire were to grow too large, the onlookers would be the first to warn their neighbor that it might get out of control or to call the authorities, not because the person in question does not have a right to do as he or she wishes on his or her own property, but because the action threatens the rights of neighbors. Similarly, the political eruptions in Grenada were deemed to be threatening by its neighbors. And just as concerned neighbors called the authorities to warn of the fire, in a similar fashion some Caribbean countries called for help from the United States. There is, however, a crucial difference in the way such a matter is handled on a personal or community level or on a state level. Any member of the community can call the fire brigade. In the affairs of state only the regional group should have such authority, as the OECS nations did.

The murder of Bishop and of so many members of his cabinet had convinced OECS leaders that it would be impossible to have a working relationship with either the military or civilian authority that might emerge. The demonstrations by former members of the cabinet and the crowds they attracted convinced these leaders that there was no order. The uncertainty over the length of this process, the possible loss of lives during it, and the demonstration effect it might have on their own institutions like the army, police, and radical political groups made their decisions inevitable.

While intervention is intervention no matter who undertakes it, recent events show a pattern evolving among regional and subregional groups that suggests a modification of the normally rigid view of this principle. The invasion of Uganda by the Republic of Tanzania to depose that country's dictator seems to have won approval from many who had become tired of the Ugandan dictator's brutality toward his own people. That the president of Tanzania, a socialist and democrat and a darling of the democratic left, should have broken with established practice and responded so radically shows a realization on his part that such butchery and barbarism cannot be tolerated within a region without debilitating and chronic consequences for one's neighbors. This is true even if it is carried out by a legally constituted government, having come to office through the process of elections. Military governments, on the other hand, pledging to preserve law and order or to forestall serious political disputes that could lead to fierce civil strife, have an even stronger imperative to display the qualities they purport to represent. That a formal decision to invade was reached by the OECS leaders and their partners in the region gives the Grenada invasion an unusual twist. Here were close associates ready to invade and inviting the help of a senior partner.

While there is support for conformity to some pattern of behavior internationally and regionally, there is an equal rejection of intervention by either of the world's two superpowers. It seems clear that the superpowers, in their rivalry, bring the kind of political baggage with them that generates immensely strong feelings both for and against their presence and obscures the real political issues.[3]

The reaction to foreign intervention, like so much in politics, is a combination of two responses, one intellectual and one emotional. One can fervently believe in a political principle and yet act contrary to that belief when self-interest is threatened. The nearer one is to the source of the problem, the more emotional the reaction, whereas distance encourages a much more intellectual response. This is why the U.S.-led invasion was so popular in the Commonwealth Caribbean region among groups who, under other circumstances, would have found such action extremely objectionable. Other groups and nations further from the scene, and possessing more sophisticated institutions to deal with upheavals, took a more Olympian view. But there is a logical reason for this response. One diplomatic historian writing nearly half a century ago noted these "two contrary tendencies" of a need by peoples to integrate for political and economic purposes, yet desiring to preserve the identity of the smaller group. He put it this way:

One prediction may be made with some confidence. The concept of sovereignty is likely to become in the future even more blurred and indistinct than it is at present. The term was invented after the break-up of the medieval system to describe the independent character of the authority claimed and exercised by states which no longer recognised even the formal overlordship of the Empire. It was never more than a convenient label; and when distinctions began to be made between political, legal and economic sovereignty or between internal and external sovereignty, it was clear that the label had ceased to perform its proper function as a distinguishing mark for a single category of phenomena. . . . It is unlikely that the future units of power will take much account of formal sovereignty. There is no reason why each unit should not consist of groups of several formally sovereign states so long as the effective (but not necessarily the nominal) authority is exercised from a single centre. The effective group unit of the future will in all probability not be the unit formally recognised as such by international law. Any project of an international order which takes these formal units as its basis seems likely to prove unreal.[4]

It was in the light of this attitude that the heads of the OECS countries presumed to make the decision that they did on behalf of a member of their group.

In the end it has to be the judgment of a few that prevails, rather than strict adherence to the law, and one can only hope that these few are right more often than not. It seems clear that the more fragile, new, struggling democracies are seeking some modification in the rules of behavior that were formulated and that worked well in a European world, a world that had shared and common experiences. Today, in a world of diverse social, economic, and regional differences, and with heightened nationalism, the rules that worked relatively well for the old order no longer seem as useful. For instance, why should a small group of men as head of the military with a handful of men loyal to them be thought of as more legitimate to govern than an official opposition party? But civilian politician have nearly no chance once the military steps in. From another standpoint, little can be done when a small strong-willed clique decides to subvert the constitutional and election process to preserve itself in power indefinitely. It may well be that we need some sort of international or regional agreement and structure to arbitrate disputes for those who need it.

The Caribbean leaders, like leaders in several other areas, have made a serious effort to fashion and build financial, political, and economic institutions necessary for development. It would be tragic if world opinion on the question of intervention remained so inflexible that elite groups, in their struggle for power, could contribute to the destabilization of a whole region and to the economic setback of millions of innocent people. The struggle for power within and between parties can be immensely divisive. Given the relatively new and fragile framework in which politicians must work, they can become easily seduced by the power they wield or frustrated when they deem that the system does not give them a fair chance at offering themselves as alternatives to the governing party. Often this quarrel among elites seeking to govern spills over into civil disorder and other lawless acts. Such an occurrence over a prolonged period only leads to a determination not to compromise. The result usually is that while the political elites play out their own minuets, the economy suffers. In today's world of complexity and competition, such events mean untold suffering for millions of people. The stakes are too high to accommodate such a luxury any longer. The outcome will be a world where changes in government could be continuous, which cannot help but severely affect even those countries that today think themselves insulated from such problems.

NOTES

1. Hugh O'Shaughnessy, *Grenada: An Eyewitness Account of the U.S. Invasion and the Caribbean History That Provoked It* (New York: Dodd, Mead and Company, 1984), p. 32.

2. Ibid., pp. 35–36.

3. Intervention by superpowers has always presented much difficulty for political theorists, even those of the eighteenth and nineteenth centuries. For a brief discussion of this dilemma, see Edward Vose Gulick, *Europe's Classical Balance of Power* (New York: W. W. Norton and Company, 1955) pp. 62–63.

4. Edward Hallett Carr, *The Twenty Years' Crisis, 1919–1939* (New York: Harper Torchbooks, 1946), pp. 203–31.

11

Conclusion

The invasion of Grenada raised a number of problems and posed a number of challenges for conventional thinkers about foreign policy and for political and military analysts. In a military sense, the campaign seemed to prove that there is no such thing as the swift surgical strike that politicians and civilian analysts speak glibly about in public forums. On the first day or two the invasion troops had a real struggle on their hands, surprising many who went into battle with cultural biases about banana republics. Although U.S. troops were fighting a poorly equipped, very disorganized Grenadian military force and Cuban construction workers with training as reserves, it is not unreasonable to conclude that luck and good timing were on the U.S. side. The campaign was not the well-oiled operation that the administration and media would have us believe.

Gone are the days when natives would freeze at the sight of troops from a developed nation with sophisticated hardware. Vietnam, Afghanistan, and Beirut stand as stark reminders that "to do nothing for real," as one writer put it, might be a pleasing policy with which to flaunt American power before Americans, but those at whom it is directed do not see it this way. As the saying goes when people meet in friendly confrontation in the Caribbean: "If you have it you've got to use it." To engage an adversary like the United States, a nation of such overwhelming might, win, lose, or draw, is an opportunity to learn and to match wits with the best. Even if you lose, you can claim victory because you have tangled with the best and the odds were against you from the beginning. So it was in Grenada. The Reagan administration, by its own admission, did not expect the resistance it encountered from the Grenadians and certainly did not expect it from the Cuban workers, given the morale of the people of the country and the domestic turmoil. The difference in philosophy in a world made small by quick communication and people willing to assert their interests calls for a response other than the conventional one used by the old order and still in use today. One observer put it this way:

> One of the distinctive facts about contemporary history is that it is world history and that the forces shaping it cannot be understood unless we are pressed to adopt world-wide perspectives; and this means not merely supplementing our conventional view of the recent past by adding a few chapters on extra-European affairs, but re-examining and revising the whole structure of assumptions and preconceptions on which that view is based. Precisely because American, African, Chinese, Indian and other branches of extra-European history cut into the past at a different angle, they cut across the traditional lines; and this very fact casts doubt on the adequacy of the old patterns and suggests the need for a new ground-plan.[1]

The failure to see Third World countries for what they are rather than what each superpower would like them to be has been partly responsible for the poor state of international relations since the end of World War II. One knowledgeable and respected former U.S. diplomat and scholar noticed the apparent sameness in policy of the two superpowers toward Third World nations. Commenting on U.S. concern for Soviet gains in the Third World, he wrote: "The Soviet leaders do indeed make efforts to gain influence and authority among the regimes and peoples of the Third World. While the methods they employ do not seem to differ greatly from those of other major powers, including us, and while their efforts in this direction have not met, generally speaking, with any very alarming measure of success, these practices naturally arouse concern and resentment in large sections of our official community."[2] Little wonder then that Third World leaders do not see as clear a difference between the policies of the superpowers as the U.S. policymakers and populace would like and think they deserve. The economic and political choices made by Bishop and the leaders of the NJM and the response of the United States to them seems to bear out this observation.

Part of the problem lies in external and internal perceptions of the superpowers vis-à-vis other states. Both superpowers perceive themselves, and quite rightly so, to be militarily and economically dominant in their spheres of influence. But is is primarily their military capability that puts them in a league above all others. While this gives their peoples and governments a sense of great power and responsibility, outsiders see this as technological power that can only be used for defensive purposes. They also perceive a superpower to be able to react only in a conventional manner when its power and authority are challenged. In acting predictably, they do not possess a major advantage except in numbers and quality of hardware. The risks to the challenger then are not overwhelmingly as great.

Politically Grenada posed many perplexing questions for the United States and the international community. Can a few countries from a subregion, believing that they all subscribe to a culture of democracy, collectively decide that internal conditions in a member state warrant military intervention? Once that decision is made, can the United States of America or any other Western democracy with the men and material refuse such an apparently reasonable request? In the face of the aggressive advances of competing ideologies over the last forty years, it would seem that Western democracies cannot afford to adhere to their traditional position of nonintervention, not because the principle itself is bad or ought not to be followed but because the events of the last thirty years have more than tripled the number of nations in the world, radically altering the dynamics of international affairs. No longer do we have a collection of European nations with a similar culture and politics. Rather, we now have competing political and social philosophies within both the more developed and the recently independent countries. While the more developed countries may be able to channel the opposition and make it productive because their social and political institutions are strong enough to contain the competition, the newer countries are more fragile and sometimes cannot. Despite their protestations of independence, perhaps these countries do need help and guidance from time to time, not only economically and financially but politically as well. Not surprisingly, this need might not be readily admitted by these countries, or even realized.

In a world of uncertainty, democratic change remains ever elusive, even for the well-prepared. The Western democracies must decide whether it is in their interest to assist countries that are desperately trying to build and foster some form of democracy, or whether ideological purity and, as one Caribbean leader put it, "unquestioning concubinage'' is what they seek. Here the case of Chile is an appropriate example. Having broken the cycle of the military overthrowing the civilian government at every point of crisis, as often happens in many Latin American states, the country enjoyed over fifty years of civilian rule. Chileans boasted of their democracy and Americans endorsed their claim. Then the people of Chile elected a Marxist government—one that was prepared to submit itself to the people for re-election at the completion of its term. Nothing was done during the intervening period to the political structure to suggest that this would not be so. However, in the economic sphere a serious effort was made to move the economy in the direction of the government's philosophy. The economic transformation did not go as planned. The poor state of the economy made many people dissatisfied, even some of the government's most ardent supporters. People took to the streets as the economy began to totter. With the encouragement of the U.S. government and private interests, the Chilean army moved in and took over. The intervention of the army rid the United States of what it considered to be the menace of the Allende government, but it killed a nation's dream, a dream that had taken generations to build and would take generations to restore. And to what avail? To most knowledgeable observers, the poor state of the economy and the government's inability to deliver on its promises to its supporters were certain to hamper its chances of re-election. If it were re-elected, its prior experience might well have caused it to change its course and give a broader representation in its economic plans. Rather than that, the people of Chile got one of the most brutal military dictatorships to appear in the hemisphere for some time. The democracy about which they had once boasted died in the ashes of the Presidential Palace. In the end, the people of Chile will have learned that it is easier to restore the economy than it is to restore representative government and civil liberties. That the United States itself could have yielded to such a temptation, not taking account of the long-term implications of its actions for democracy, suggests either a genuine lack of understanding of what is at stake, a contempt for such countries, or a mistaken belief that only it and a few other Western countries are really capable of supporting democratic institutions and surviving in the midst of revolutions and disorder.

The ideologies of the two superpowers complement each other remarkably well, one eager to welcome anyone who would join it, the other claiming exclusive membership. But exclusivity is not a sound policy in today's world. In some countries many of the exclusive clubs of the colonial expatriates fell very quickly on hard times after independence precisely because they had been exclusive for so long that no one in the new order wanted to be identified with them. Similarly, the affluent and democratic West can seek to understand and aid some of the developments in Third World countries or it can remain smug about its own good fortune.

This is not to say that there are not serious problems within many Third World countries. There can be no doubt that many in the modernizing middle class in these countries are socialists and use Marxist rhetoric to attack American economic and cultural expansionism. But the Marxist rhetoric they use only provides a convenient structure and coherence for various grievances and is congenial to those who regard themselves as victims or underdogs.[3] As a result, many social and political proposals and criticisms are couched in a Marxist rhetoric that offends many in the West. Nevertheless, it is a form of speech, explanation, and analysis used by large numbers of intellectuals and has become a "form of conventional wisdom, especially in academic settings and its subculture."[4] While the language of many Third World modernizers is at odds with that of many policymakers in the West, especially those in the United States, their aspirations and goals are not as different as they seem. Many of these academicians, while expressing admiration for revolutionaries like Castro, Mao, Ho Chi Minh, and others because of their defiance of U.S. and Western economic and political power and because of their achievements in social welfare, are not prepared to live under that kind of political system.[5] This attitude reflects the "recognition of the constraints on free expression that prevail" under those systems.[6] Most regard the United States as a benign power that they can influence by their actions and language and see the Soviets more as a malignant power with a fixed notion of how life should be lived.

In this period of readjustment and restructuring of the world economy, an excellent opportunity exists for a meaningful dialogue between all groups from most parts of the world. No longer is talk from Third World modernizers dominated by politics; economics now plays a big part in discussions of their plight. Indeed, former Prime Minister Michael Manley of Jamaica readily admitted at a recent conference that his democratic socialist party had made many mistakes politically and vowed to correct these, but he laid great stress on the fact that the commercial interests of his country had been as great a failure, if not more, because of their unwillingness to take the risks necessary to transform themselves from "importing merchants to domestic manufacturers" over the last twenty years of independence. It was an important transformation that he claimed the parties had neglected and that needed to be addressed. He stressed that there was a "patriotic private sector" that he said should not be condemned out of hand.[7] This recognition of the need to actively encourage and develop a commercial sector does not meant accepting the free enterprise model of the United States or the West, but it does show that a search for ideas and answers is on the way and that the West has every chance of influencing the eventual results. This is what politics is all about: the alignment and realignment of groups and the search for solutions that work. It is in this sense that the press can serve as a conduit for the flow of ideas in both directions. Much of the Western press, and that of the United States in particular, is seen as nationalistic, giving prominence to bureaucratic disputes and differences in ideas among U.S. and Western policymakers, most of whom come from the same background and tend to differ mostly in degree, so that what appears to be a dialogue is actually a monologue. Reporting on Grenada was no different.

The refusal of the U.S. press to report contradictory facts as boldly as it did Reagan's assertions was due to the fact that many members of the press shared some of the same biases as the president, especially from the standpoint of U.S. hegemony in the world. The result is that declarations of the independence of the press by U.S. journalists and their organizations are seen in the Third World as just so much hot air, given the results. As a result of its own bias, the U.S. press, by not reporting all of the facts, took the position that the president was right and that no effort would be made to disprove his allegations.

As has been noted, the Reagan administration had no great love for Maurice Bishop and actively opposed his government. Regardless of whether the position Reagan took toward the NJM was misguided or not, he had to deal with a totally different situation once Bishop and his cabinet were killed and the OECS request was received. Intervention became a short-term policy to halt a deteriorating situation. It did not imply a change of posture in the Reagan administration toward other present or future governments with the same orientation as Bishop. Not surprisingly, many people could agree with the decision to undertake the Grenada invasion, but severely differed with other aspects of the administration's foreign policy.

However, the Reagan administration did not use the opportunity to try to convince its allies that Western democracies had to begin to think differently about military assistance to nations that actually request it. The administration could have justified the invasion with the real reason of a legitimate request to come to the assistance of the OECS states. Rather, by using the welfare of the students and a Communist takeover as an excuse for mounting the invasion, the administration damaged its credibility and betrayed its real motives for joining the invasion.

The administration may have missed an opportunity to convince its stronger allies that a new era in foreign policy demanded a more flexible view of the laws and that such allowances are made in response to genuine requests for assistance. The essential difference between a genuine request for help and intervention is that the latter is undertaken by an outside power solely to achieve political ends that suit its interests. The result is the installation of a government chosen by or closely allied to the invading country. Intervention by consent, on the other hand, is undertaken to prevent prolonged squabbles among elite groups that could result in the concentration of the economy in the hands of a few and the emergence of an oppressive oligarchy. It does not seek to install any one group in power. This decision is left to the people of the country, supervised by the regional or subregional organization to which the nation belongs. It is a recognition by the superpower that its role has changed and that it is willing to support other middle powers and subregional groups that will decide how orderly change will come into being.

In modern times the simple brandishing of power, even by a superpower, does not particularly frighten many leaders. Even in unpopular governments, overtly offensive acts by superpowers can serve as a rallying point to mobilize the nation against invaders. More importantly, a superpower needs an enlightened foreign policy that is embraced by the small nation. It is America's embrace of brute force and the apparent neglect of negotiation that has caused so many to question so often the approach of the Reagan administration in dealing with international disputes.

The strength of the West, and the United States in particular, lies in its credibility, and that remains high even in those Third World countries that often condemn it. Unlike the Soviet Union, the strength of the

West and Japan for the developing countries does not lie in military preparedness but in their superior economic strength, ranging from advanced technology to superior farming techniques. It lies in holding out access to these, to the markets that can use them, and to the financing to develop them.[8]

While it is true that the Soviet Union, through its generous military assistance program to many Third World countries, has indirectly had a hand in deciding the outcome of internal factional conflicts like those in Angola and Ethiopia, a prolonged close association with the Soviets has left them and others before them dissatisfied with the paucity of economic and technological assistance they have received. They lament the lack of growth in their economies, especially in the area of international trade. This restricts their international maneuverability and standing and tarnishes their hopes for some degree of real economic progress.

The theme here is that the United States must accommodate itself in the near future to a new distribution of power in the world. Western Europe, Japan, and the newly industrialized nations of the Third World are playing much larger roles in international economic matters than they did a decade ago. This diffusion of economic power in the international system places new constraints on the exercise of U.S. policy and poses new challenges for her hegemony. It therefore makes even a superpower like the United States more dependent on its allies in executing policy. A number of embryonic developments show that some sort of fragile mechanism has taken root and could be developed. In the case of the Caribbean, the regional groups, the Associated States, and Caricom acted collectively if not in complete unity to try to resolve what was occurring in Grenada. The motivation was that whatever happened in Grenada would have an impact on them all, and the situation had degenerated to the point where outside assistance was necessary to bring all parties to negotiations. This has been attempted in other regions of the world without the same result but with the same intent. The Organization of African States has attempted without success to mediate several domestic disputes. In Latin America the interested parties in the Central American area came together as the Contadora Group to formulate proposals to try to stop hostilities within the Central American area. These modest and varied efforts could be strengthened in a number of ways. But they would be dependent on the exclusion of the superpowers from any regional grouping, while realizing that they maintain a political interest in the eventual outcome.

It should be left, then, to regional groups to decide and recommend how a nation within that region should be dealt with. The regional organization decides on the steps any government coming to power should take to be welcomed into the group. Not that a particular country and its government should be excluded from the family of nations, but a distinction must be made between the country and its administration. The more developed Western countries could assist in this process by making sure that aid and all current contact is maintained with a government, but disallowing its head of government from attending all international conferences and making any official visits to Western countries until he or she comes to some agreement with his or her regional counterparts. This insures that the people of a particular country will not be punished economically, since aid is continued but not increased, and since ministers of that government travel to conferences, but their head of government is left isolated. Such an arrangement would make regional groupings responsible for their security and for dealing with revolutionary, military, and other leaders who might emerge. Proximity can have a sobering effect on political decisions in which one's self-interest is involved and can free the United States from some of the burden of seeming to be the world's policeman. If help is needed from a larger nation to deal with a problem, there would be some regional consensus for such action.

The United States itself could take the initiative by announcing that it would treat all of its allies alike. This means that the president, vice president, and secretary of state, in travelling to any country, would insist on having at least a publicized visit with the main opposition members. Thus the government in the host nation would be forced to acknowledge some opposition, no matter how small and disorganized. But much more, the United States itself would be in touch with opposition groups and not be caught making hasty overtures to such groups when a bad situation has already begun to deteriorate and its influence is minimal, as was the case in Iran and Nicaragua. Such an approach by both the United States and its allies will at least provide some prominence for alternative opinions without necessarily encouraging them. Finally, governments that look with displeasure on and forbid such contacts, rather than being the allies they claim to be, sooner or later force the United States to act in the political interest of the then head of government rather than in its own interest, which eventually damages U.S. credibility and does not serve its interest. In all instances, a firm insistence that a democratic nation maintain contact with both a government and its opposition is in keeping with U.S. opinion and principle and can give life to struggling opposition in some repressive societies. This would also strengthen the role of the United States in world affairs as well as its prestige without weakening any preference it might have for one party over another.

The well-advertised wealth and prosperity of the United States has advantages and constraints that must be acknowledged. Once involved in a crisis, the United States engenders not only hope for a solution, but perhaps more importantly, hope for economic progress to follow. As a result, a number of undercurrents begin to ensue, some powered by those who feel that their cause is just and that they deserve to win, others by those who know that they are in a position to take advantage of the coming new order. In such instances sons of the upwardly mobile go into the army as officers and into a range of occupations that afford them travel study trips overseas. But this is a group that allies itself with whoever is in power. Their ambition is known and they are generally distrusted, even though their professional skills are necessary for development. In other words, they are perceived as looking for opportunity rather than having nationalist commitment; they demand pay and titles for their work. Meanwhile, the more nationalist, sometimes ideological, groups have only their zeal and hope for the future to galvanize them. It is nationalism and zeal that holds the Russian army at bay in Afghanistan and that defeated U.S. attempts to find a popular and effective government to install in South Vietnam. It has also seen U.S.-trained armies disintegrate in Iran and Beirut, Lebanon.

In very few countries in the Third World have the moderates been able to gain political stature. As a result, the United States is severely handicapped when it becomes involved in the political affairs of another country and tries to find the middle ground. The policy of the middle ground often supports the status quo, then rushes to implore the friendly governments to make concessions only after the situation has reached the point of heightened violence. It is a policy that is committed to change only after the government has suffered severe reverses from an opposition that has been savaged too often to settle for less than total victory.

This policy has on many occasions left the U.S. government looking on helplessly as events abroad over which it once had much influence, get completely out of hand. It is a policy that has caused much internal discord in the U.S. body politic itself as policymakers and political activists rage over who is to be blamed for the latest debacle and as the general public becomes once again demoralized over the loss of U.S. influence and the vehemence with which the new groups show their displeasure for U.S. power and policy.

There are those who argue that it is naive to assume that the United States has any serious interest in helping developing countries—U.S. policy is carefully calculated, good old-fashioned exploitation. They would argue that certainly Third World nations would like to be seen for what they are rather than what each superpower would like them to be, but that the sad truth is that Third World nations are of little or no value to anyone; they must be shaped into something of value for one or the other superpower or they will languish, if not perish altogether. They would further assert that both that United States and the USSR realize this, and that this is why Third World leaders see no clear difference in their policies. They could conclude by arguing that it is naive of Third World leaders to refuse to play along in a game that is the only game in town, and they suffer for it.

This is a valid and convincing argument. But it only holds water when there is strong political control from the center that could be backed by economic and other sanctions. In today's world, where the military component of power no longer is the deterrent it once was, and where the United States no longer enjoys the economic supremacy it once did, executing policy becomes even more difficult. For as has happened in the recent past, U.S. economic sanctions have seen her allies rush in to fill the void. This sort of economic competition is only likely to intensify and will spread to the armaments area in the near future. This severely reduces the effectiveness U.S. policy is likely to have abroad.

What then is the position of these realists? Acting as a big power should be passé; it is an argument heavy with nostalgia. It, like Ronald Reagan, says there existed a simpler, better time and I want to return to it. It is an argument that has already been overtaken by technological, economic, and political change, but is nonetheless often invoked— political and economic follies played out for a local audience.

The realists, by supporting the traditional way in which things were done by former great powers, often lose sight of modern developments. They tend to support the system as it is and seldom make recommendations for change without being goaded. Therefore, over the last two decades we have seen serious conflict arise between the ideas and the politics of the governing elite and the population. The consistent response to any petition for domestic change has been the same. No matter who the petitioners are and irrespective of their ideology, the retort has been the same: they are Communist; they are small; they have no support. This simple formula has made the difference between reason and inflexibility, reform and revolution. It shows that even reasonable men when in power tend to act in an unreasonable manner to protect their power most of the time.

In the future, U.S. administrations should be much more willing to work with governments as they are constituted, whether democratic or socialist, without abandoning its own ideals. This means that they must take a much broader view of developments in Third World countries and see the possibilities for change, rather than paying strict attention to their rhetoric and posturing.

NOTES

1. Geoffrey Barraclough, *An Introduction to Contemporary History* (London: Penguin Books, 1967), p. 10.

2. George Kennan, "Reflections: Breaking The Spell," *New Yorker*, October 3, 1983, p. 45.

3. Paul Hollander, "Radical Chic Is Status Quo among Mexican Intellectuals," *Wall Street Journal*, August 17, 1984, p. 15.

4. Ibid.

5. Ibid.

6. Ibid.

7. Michael Manley, Address to the Conference—New Perspectives on Caribbean Studies: Toward the 21st Century and Prospects for Caribbean Basin Integration, August 28-September 1, 1984.

8. Henry Bienen, "Let's Use U.S. Edge in Africa," *New York Times*, July 13, 1983, p. A21.

Selected Bibliography

Almond, G. A., and Coleman, eds. *The Politics of Developing Areas*. Princeton: Princeton University Press, 1960.

Apter, David E. *The Politics of Modernization*. Chicago: University of Chicago Press, 1965.

Augier, F. R., and S. Gordon. *Sources of West Indian History*. London: Longman, 1968.

Augier, R., et al. *The Making of the West Indies*. London: Longman, 1960.

Ayearst, Morley. *The British West Indies: The Search for Self Government*. London: Allen and Unwin, 1960.

Barraclough, Geoffrey. *An Introduction to Contemporary History*. New York: Penguin Books, 1967.

Bell, Wendell, ed. *The Democratic Revolution in the West Indies*. Massachusetts: Schenkman Publishing Co., 1966.

Bell, Wendell. *Jamaican Leaders: Political Attitudes in a New Nation*. Berkeley: University of California Press, 1964.

Brogan, D. W. *The American Character*. New York: Vintage Books, 1956.

Calleo, David P. *The Imperious Economy*. Cambridge: Harvard University Press, 1982.

Caroll, Peter N. *It Seemed Like Nothing Happened: The Tragedy and Promise of America in 1970*. New York: Holt Rinehart & Winston, 1982.

Carr, E. H. *The Twenty Years Crisis 1919–1939: An Introduction to the Study of International Relations*. New York: Harper & Row, 1964.

Carr, E. H. *Nationalism and After*. London: Macmillan, 1945.

Dutt, R. P. *The Crisis of Britain and the British Empire*. London: Lawrence and Wishart, 1953.

Duverger, Maurice. *Political Parties*. London: Methuen, 1954.

Frankel, Joseph. *The Making of Foreign Policy: An Analysis of Decisionmaking*. Oxford University Press, 1963.

Gabriel, Richard A. *Military Incompetence: Why the American Military Doesn't Win*. New York: Hill & Wang, 1985.

Gordon, S.A. *Century of West Indian Education*. London: Longman, 1963.

Gulick, Edward Vose. *Europe's Classical Balance of Power*. New York: W. W. Norton & Company, 1955.

Hodgson, Godfrey. *America in Our Time: From World War II to Nixon—What Happened and Why*. New York: Vintage Books, 1978.

Kennan, George. *The Nuclear Delusion: Soviet American Relations in the Atomic Age*. New York: Pantheon Books, 1983.

Lewis, Gordon K. *The Growth of the Modern West Indies*. London: MacGibbon & Kee, 1968.

Morganthau, Hans. *Political Among Nations*. New York: Alfred J. Knopf, 1961.

Morris, Charles R. *A Time of Passion: America 1960–1980*. New York: Penguin Books, 1986.

Moser, Charles, ed. *Combat on Communist Territory*. Regency Gateway, Inc. Free Congress Research & Education Foundation, 1985.

O'Shaughnessy, Hugh. *Grenada: An Eyewitness Account of the U.S. Invasion and Caribbean History That Provoked It*. New York: Dodd Mead & Company, 1984.

Parry, J. H., and Philip A. Shorlock, *A Short History of the West Indies*. London: Macmillan Press Ltd., 1980.

Snyder, Richard C., H. W. Bruck, and Burton Sapin, eds. *Foreign Policy Decisionmaking: An Approach to the Study of International Politics*. New York: The Free Press, 1962.

Stockwell, John. *In Search of Enemies: A CIA Story*. New York: W. W. Norton & Company, 1978.

Reports

The Commonwealth Regional Secretariat, from Carifta to the Caribbean Community.

Report of the Duffus Commission of Enquiry into the Breakdown of Law and Order and Police Brutality in Grenada, 1975.

House of Commons Second Report from the Foreign Affairs Committee on Grenada. Her Majesty's Stationary Office, March 1984.

Grenada: A Preliminary Report. Washington, D.C.: U.S. Departments of State and Defense, 1983.

Grenada Documents: An Overview and Selection. Washington, D.C.: U.S. Departments of State and Defense, 1984.

Forward Ever: Three Years of the Grenadian Revolution. Sidney: Pathfinder Press, 1982.

Index

About the Author

REYNOLD A. BURROWES is a commodity floor specialist with Dean Witter Reynolds. He is the author of *The Wild Coast: An Account of Politics in Guyana*.